Troubled Co

TROUBLED
COLLIERIES 2

Troubled Collieries

First Published in England in the United Kingdom
In the year 2002. Reprinted 2004 including the stories of
Seaham, Brancepeth Wingate & East Hetton (Kelloe) Collieries
Bermac Publications
Newton Aycliffe,
www.bermac.co.uk
E/Mail books@bermac.co.uk
01325-311956

© Bernard McCormick 2002 & 2004

All rights reserved. No part of this publication
May be reproduced, or stored in a retrieval system.
Nor transmitted in any form, Electronic or mechanical. It can not be
recorded or photocopied or used in any other way without prior permission
of the Publisher or copyright holder.

ISBN 0-9541756-5-4

Typeset in 11pt Times New Roman
Titles in Vineta B.T. & Tiffany HV BT
Typesetting and originating by
Bermac Publications.
Printed and Bound in Great Britain
BY MACDONALD PRESS LIMITED, TUDHOE.

TROUBLED COLLIERIES 2

BY

Bernard McCormick

Bermac Publications
(Newton Aycliffe)

BIBLIOGRAPHY

The Death Pit	Forster
Explosion At Easington	Gavin Jones Purdon
Sacriston Mine Disaster	Gavin Jones Purdon
An Account of the Explosion at Felling	Hodgson
Mines and Miners	Simonin
Explosions in Coal Mines	W.N.&J.B. Atkinson
The Hartley Colliery Disaster	John Elliott McCutcheon
Great Pit Disasters	Baron Duckham
The Memoir of Hartley Accident	T. Wemyss Reid
Memoir Hartley	T.E. Forester
Newcastle Daily Journal	
Northern Echo	
Yorkshire Post	
Brancepeth Colliery	Frank Gent
Wingate	William A. Moyes
Troubled Seams	John Elliott McCutcheon

To the many miners in my life

PREFACE

During the eighteenth century hundreds of miners lost their lives by explosion, roof falls and other accidents in order to develop the coal industry in England, as the main power source in the Country; as well as a major export commodity to gain precious currency abroad. In the Collieries, which I have written, there were in excess of, 1200 deaths. Small accidents in the pit were normal and did not attract much press attention, even when fatalities occurred. However these fatalities were noticed when the banners were draped in black at the annual Durham Big Meeting onlookers made special note of these pits.

Each Colliery disaster made coal owners re-think safety but they did not always implement change; except after Hartley when, with the help of William Coulson the one shaft system was outlawed. For years experts pointed to coal dust as being the major factor in the travel of the blast, in an explosion; the force of the blast died out where there was no coal dust, especially near to shafts, and explosions never occurred in wet or damp seams. On trying to find books to research mining disasters I found nearly all were out of print; even in public libraries they were in short supply. I have attempted to redress this situation in a small way by writing this book; like the men who lost their lives in the two main world wars, and are remembered each year, it is only right and proper that the men who lost their lives in the mines, should also be remembered. Without them we would not have been able to survive as a Country, during both wars; as we needed the coal industry for the power to run the factories, and to supply the heat for the home front. These brave men should be fresh in our thoughts and memories, for the debt we owe them, for our present prosperity.

As the years went by, the industry was taken over by the 'National Coal Board', workers and families in the industry sighed a sigh of relief, thinking that the safe running of the pits would be paramount and that unsafe working conditions would not be tolerated; this alas was not the case and on 29th. May 1951 there was a terrible explosion at 'Easington Colliery', Co. Durham, when 81 miners and two rescuers lost their lives. This explosion could have been prevented if the powers that be had observed and acted on, the danger signs that were obvious at the time. The Duckbill District, part of the 'Five Quarter Seam' was known to be dusty;

the coal being transported by belts. In the days prior to the disaster a check had been made when a high percentage of gas had been observed, and reported. Spiral Alarms could not be carried as they constantly sounded off. *It was obvious that even with the National Coal Board, they had not learnt the lesson on the travel of explosions, because of the presence of gas and Coal dust in the air!! In this millennium year coal dust has left another major problem when thousand's of ex-miners are dying from emphysema and other related lung diseases, when the present Labour Government has delayed the compensation payout. If it had been compulsory to wear masks when working in dusty seams this problem would not have arisen.*

Some of the stories are sad, but most show the tremendous courage of the miners and rescuers faced with death when trying to rescue their fellow men. All miners faced possible death or injury on a daily basis, especially in the years prior to 1900. I hope this book goes some way to give the miners the recognition they deserve.

March 2004 The book has for some time, been out of print; when writing the book in 2002; I regretted not including Seaham Colliery, Brancepeth, East Hetton (Kelloe) & Wingate. The miners from these areas had tremendously sad memories, while making a living at their particular Collieries, many loosing their lives in the explosions which occurred. I decided to reproduce the book and include the story of Seaham Colliery, Kelloe, Brancepeth and Wingate. A lot of my Information for 'Brancepeth', was taken from information supplied by Mr Frank Gent, who's Great Uncle lost his life at Brancepeth. Frank went to live at Middlesborough later in his life. His book was patiently written in longhand and now has a hardback cover with the headings in gold embossed writing. I have handled this book with the care it deserves and I feel that like all other information on our mining roots Franks book which is based at Willington Library will be too precious to lend out in the future and therefore will not be available. That is mainly my reason for including these Collieries; this information should be available to all. Since the first Publication in 2002 there has also been a dramatic improvement in Miners effected by Chest problems. Payouts are now progressing smoothly; with the help of Mr. Hopper and his colleagues at the NUM Headquarters, Flass Street, Durham. This is also where chest problems are assessed.

B. McCormick:

Troubled Collieries

LIST OF CONTENTS

Select Bibliography
Foreword

Chapter 1	Hartley(Northumberland)
Chapter 2	Royal Oak(Barnsley)
Chapter 3	Seaham Colliery (Durham)
Chapter 4	Senghenydd (Wales)
Chapter 5	Tudhoe(Durham)
Chapter 6	West Stanley(Durham)
Chapter 7	SacristonVictoria(Durham)
Chapter 8	Felling Colliery (Gateshead)
Chapter 9	Trimdon Grange(Durham)
Chapter 10	Easington Colliery(Durham)
Chapter 11	Brancepeth (Durham)
Chapter 12	Wingate (Durham)
Chapter 13	East Hetton (Kelloe Durham)

Some photographs of Tudhoe, Kelloe, Easington & Trimdon by the Author.

THE HARTLEY DISASTER
1862

In 1862 a disaster in a one-shaft colliery changed coal mining in England forever. 204 men and boys lost their lives in a terrible tragedy at Hartley Colliery. The beam of the pumping engine, which weighed 42 tons suddenly snapped in two; half of it falling down the pit shaft entombing all of the miners below, except for three men out of eight, travelling to the surface who were saved by no less than a miracle.

The mine was Hartley Colliery, a one shaft pit sank in 1845 by William Coulson (Master Sinker) by this date 1862 he had sank 84 mine shafts and a vast amount of sample drillings in both Northumberland and Durham. Being so successful he had gathered around him a very experienced band of sinkers. Everyone a professional sinker in his own right, among them his own son William (Billy) and Geordie Emerson his right hand man. Billy Shields, Davy Wilkinson, these were the men that arrived at the Colliery on that bleak and cold day and offered their services to try and save the entombed unfortunate men.

William Coulson was known not only in Northumberland and Durham as an expert in the field of sinking; but throughout the continent and here, was a man who was without equal the most experienced sinker in the Country offering his, and his men's services. Although Coulson was at that time getting on in years his services were readily accepted, if any one could get the men out, he could. The task of attempting to rescue the men commenced with great speed. The task itself was fraught with danger, but danger was the sinkers life and they lived with it, on a daily basis. For this reason maybe most sinkers were as it happened very religious men, mostly primitive Methodists and lay readers who could preach as well as they could sink. The day of the disaster was Thursday 16th January. 1862, the day now was Friday 17th January. This was the day that William Coulson took on the mammoth task of trying to free the unfortunate miners, it wasn't so much the task, but the enormous responsibility of being answerable to the families of the entombed men this wasn't all, there were also agitators to contend with, these also, were very evident at the pit head among other worried relations Coulson and his men indeed, were very brave men. The work to clear the shaft progressed very slowly on that Friday the sinkers toiled in shifts, all of the weekend at times going without meals. The first task was to clear the bent and broken cages from within the shaft, this together with other wreckage. The people that were rescued alive, from the mangled wreckage of the cages, were very fortunate indeed.

On that fateful Thursday morning eight men were being drawn up the shaft towards the surface when the accident happened, five of the men suffered a tragic death, whilst three managed to escape death by no less than a whisker. When one ponders over the wreckage of the cage and taking into account the massive cast iron part of the engine weighing twenty one tons and the narrow shaft any saving of life from it would seem impossible. The names of the dead were Robert Bewick, William Brown, Ralph Robson, George Sharpe (aged 16 years). The survivors were Ralph Robinson, William Sharpe and Thomas Watson. The three rescued men were imprisoned in the shaft for twelve hours.

There were very conflicting stories regarding this period within the shaft, one story in particular was that a strange light was apparent at one time. One of the men Tom Watson was a deeply religious man and respected throughout Hartley so there was no reason to disclaim the light episode. That particular morning Tom was not in much of a hurry to come away from his work after being relieved by his mate who would progress the work he had been doing, Tom was a hewer and the putter of that following shift was busy changing the full tub with a empty tub. Tom and the putter exchanged light hearted barter, obviously touching on religion knowing Tom was religious, mentioning New Jerusalem and Jordan, and joking he *wished he could get carried.* Harry Gibson was the putter; Tom was due to ride at 10 am having started his shift around 2am that morning. It was now well after his riding time and he set out nonchalantly to walk to the shaft before riding to the surface, little did he realise that he would very nearly meet his maker on that horrible day.

Harry Gibson the putter was destined to help his fellow men while entombed, offering prayers and comforting other entombed men. This testimony according to James Amour (the back shift overman) in the notes, which he left. Tom Watson arrived at the shaft and proceeded to ride for bank in the bottom deck, the following information was given to the coroner at the inquest by Tom. *"There was a sudden crack and a tremendous crush of stuff, timber and stones kept falling about the cage and we made up our minds that the shaft was closed"*. The facts were, that four corner hanging chains by which the cage was held had been snapped, half of the cage load had been thrown down the shaft this being eight men the other three had been forced to hang on to the slanting bottom of the cage. After the initial shock the survivors tried to come to terms with what had happened and just how dangerous their immediate position was.

Every thing was in complete darkness but slowly they became aware of their precarious position. They were all hanging on for dear life, Tom Watson was now hanging half out of the cage, William Sharpe was desperately hanging on for dear life. 'Old Sharpe' was still hanging on but he had sustained a very bad injury to one of his legs. There had been three Sharpe's in the cage at the outset William Sharpe managed to get a match out of his pocket whilst Tom Watson produced a candle from his pocket this to try and see exactly their position, but the water dropping down the shaft (no pump) rapidly extinguished the light. There came a cry from Old Sharpe, "*lord have mercy on us*" and Watson reflecting later said indeed God did have mercy.

Tom Watson on feeling around the position felt two ropes from the rapping wire (signal wire) to stop and start the cage. At that time cries were heard from below where the others had fallen. Old Sharpe recognized one of the voices as that of his son, who had fallen from the cage on to the wreckage below, and he tried to find means to get to him, but he was badly handicapped with his injured leg, so Tom Watson said he would try to get to him. Using the rapper wire he descended to the injured men it was a precarious decent at any time, he too could plunge to his death, but he reached the men where he was met with moans, and the sounds of men breathing their last.

Tom reached out, and his hand brushed the face of the boy George Sharpe who was half buried in the wreckage, Tom attempted to pull him out but to no avail. Tom heard other moans further over and recognized it has his brother in law Bob Bewick. Young George asked in earnest where his father was, and Tom assured him he was safe and it appeared to help a little. Young George and Tom prayed to god and then they sang a hymn, this brought thoughts of his cottage home in Hartley where his four motherless children waited for him. Tom was everything to them as their mother and his wife had died in childbirth 5 months previously his thoughts were collected and again concentrated on the Hymn and poor George.

It was now several hours since the cage had plunged down the shaft, and now the boy and also Bewick were breathing their last, Tom again concentrated a while on his own situation, his clothes were soaking wet, and he shivered with cold as he gathered his thoughts. He was becoming weaker by the minute, but still holding on to the rapper wire, he had nearly passed out twice and then it happened. Suddenly the wet murky dark shaft was illuminated as if to show the spirit leaving young Sharpe and Bewick; at the time Tom thought that he was hallucinating caused by the present situation, but a great light shone in the shaft. It seemed strange that this had happened at the very moment the two men had died, but Tom explained later that he was aware of a great presence of God at that time.

He estimated the time to be in the region of 5 PM and he had came down the pit at 2.30 am so that he had been in the pit for no less than 14 hours and infact it would be a further six hours before he was rescued. What the light did infact do, was to show him a ledge in the side of the shaft which enabled him to rest a while out of the way of the falling stone and water this allowed him to gather his strength for the further accent of the shaft to safety. After a while Tom felt it was time for a further attempt to get out of the shaft and this time he decided to concentrate on the pipes leading from the pump, but he found that this was even worse than the rapper wire so he decided to wait for the rescue which he was sure would come. After what seemed an eternity Tom heard the sounds of hammering from above, rescuers had came down the staple to the High Main seam and were trying to reach them from there.

A voice rang out from above, a sound which was the most welcome in the world rang out again 'Hello' the voice was acknowledged and again the voice rang out "how many are you" to which the reply was "four". A rope was passed down to the men from a person named Milburn they had decided to try and get the men out by using a jack rope. The rope appeared attached to a lantern. First to go was old Sharpe his leg was giving him great pain, and he was too tired to hang on, one of the others grabbed hold and clamped the old man safely, but old Sharpe still fell out of the loop he fell with a thud to where Watson was, and he died instantly. They used a better method of getting the men out after that, this was done by using a hand rope. The next was Billy Sharpe but Billy nearly never made it, he finally got hold of the rope and tied his neckerchief onto the rope this helped him to get to the surface. Ralph Robinson was next to go and there were no problems. Finally it was Watson's turn by this time Tom's limbs were numb, he was soaking wet and he was very much all in. He had scarcely got into the loop and started to rise when the side of the shaft caved in.

There was water everywhere. It was a very precarious job getting him to the surface there were new obstacles to face like broken timbers, all of the time the ascent was marred by water, but at last he reached the High Main Seam and from there out of that fated shaft just in time as he collapsed with just no energy left at all into the waiting arms of the rescuers. This was twelve hours after his descent on that fateful day. Tom Watson was put to bed in a pit house near the pit to have a welcome rest after his dreadful ordeal. When he awoke his father was sat with him; His mind relived the nightmare experienced by Tom which he had been delivered from, and which Tom attributed to God saying to his father *"oh, father, what a blessed thing religion is!"*

He clasped he's hands together and prayed like he had never prayed before, and picking an appropriate verse from the scriptures he said out loud.
"He brought me up out of a horrible pit, out of the miry clay and set my feet upon a rock. And he hath put a new song in my mouth, even praise unto our god".

Saturday 18th. 1862

Clearing the broken cage slowed the work down dramatically, especially after it was found that timber was jammed together. The timbers were reduced to small pieces and transported to bank in Corves. There was a constant fear of stone coming away from the shaft and this had to be shored up for this reason with new timbers, to make the shaft safe; work would progress on this, throughout the rescue operations. Coulson decided to concentrate on the side of the shaft where the pump pipes were, hoping that at this side the debris would not be as bad as other areas, but as the holes were made through, they were filled in by other debris, the men worked round the clock all in the same mind, aiming for the quick release of the poor stricken miners. At that position Coulson estimated that they were 30 feet from the yard seam and the unfortunate miners. On Monday 20th there was great hope that they might find a gap near the furnace drift leading to the yard seam, this gave everyone great hope and the sinkers renewed their effort and toiled on relentlessly, to reach this point. But hope turned to despair when without notice there was a new danger, which would play a major part in the rescue attempt, and this was gas. In fact Coulson's son was badly gassed, and had to get medical treatment from the medical staff.

The gas was seen near the hole where the water pipes were situated at first it appeared as scythe in vapor form, the sinkers began showing symptoms of sickness and nausea it was plain to see that they were being gassed, their lights were also burning brighter and it was decided that the gas was Carbonic oxide gas which was lethal, the sinkers had came across it many times in the past when winning shafts. On Tuesday the sinkers reached the pumping scaffold, which was their object, but on the removal of a large beam the gas spurted out with much force, just like a giant gusher. The men working on that particular shift were greatly affected by the gas and just managed to get to the surface. The men working in the High main seam were also greatly affected and were brought out very ill indeed.

Staple (Alternative small escape route to a higher seam)

There was a staple leading from the yard seam to the Low Main and it was correctly assumed that the back shift overman would lead the men through the staple into the low main, which they did. Coulson and his men were fully aware of the implications of this now that gas was involved. They feared for the lives of the entombed men and also their own lives, they were in no doubt that they were dealing with a killer. Coulson did much soul searching on that day and did not want to lose any more lives in the confined space of the shaft. He regretted the prescence of gas and feared for the entombed men and the rescuers. He decided and quite rightly so, that the shaft would have to be properly ventilated before any more progress could be made on the shaft clearing. He very much sympathized with the entombed men and also their families waiting at the pithead, but he knew in his heart that this must be done. He was responsible to the sinker's wives and families among them his own son, and he could not make any mistakes,

Coulson was very brave when he took on this task, and he accepted full and unequivocal responsibility for it. As a 'Master Sinker', this had been the procedure right through his career and he had always accepted this responsibility, he had to make instant decisions, which would always have a very large influence on him and the men working with him, and also the thousands of people depending on his judgment for their livelihoods. A temporary partition was made for the shaft, using a brattice cloth fastened with battens supplies of the brattice (*material to divide the shaft to create movement of air*) was in very short supply, and supplies were quickly arranged with Seaham Colliery, where it was plentiful & quickly dispatched, this had caused a delay of twenty four hours. It was no easy job fixing the brattice but the job was finally completed, creating a downcast on one side assisted by an artificial water fall, the foul air was drawn up the other side through the high main seam, through the staple via. The engine house, the foul air drawn by the fires in the engine house, and finally out into the atmosphere through the engine house chimney.

Protest:

Late on Monday evening the crowd at the pit head started to get very agitated, they intimated that everything was not being done to rescue their loved ones and friends who were trapped. Coulson reassured them that this was not the case, and indeed everything humanly possible was being done to secure the trapped miners. He also told them that they were pushing ahead as fast as possible, Coulson went on further to say that as long as there was no scythe in the pit then the miners were perfectly okay but he further said that there was in fact some scythe in the pit. Coulson stood before the crowd dressed in his protective shaft clothing, with back skin and leather hat, which was glistening with the water from the shaft, his care worn face showed genuine concern for the wives family and friends of the entombed miners, and people knew that Coulson was doing everything humanly possible in order to get the unfortunate miners out and back to their loved one's and they knew that if anyone could, this man would succeed but they also knew that he was very much up against it.

At this time he told them firmly but carefully what he intended to do in the next few hours in order to free the poor miners. For all this the agitators within the crowd still would not accept it, but at this time Coulson had a brainwave and he informed the crowd that if they wished they could nominate two people from within their numbers who could go into the shaft and report back to the others on the progress being made by Coulson and his men, and this was accepted. Two men were appointed and sent down the shaft but there was some delay in them returning and the crowd, again became restless, and they were really in a foul mood. They shouted, "where are the two men", and were told that they had still not returned, eventually they did return, and their comments made the crowd even worse. One of the men stood in front of the crowd, he said that there was no scythe in the shaft but there was a lot of water, further questions and answers were exchanged with the sinkers and it was finally decided that reports would be given every two hours on the scythe and also the general progress. A high-pitched voice rang out and broke the silence "are they still alive", this was rubbished by the rest, and a man said how would they know that woman, the crowd was now rather subdued. Most of the woman had been at the pit head since the crisis had unfolded and they were very tired indeed, and worry for their loved one's were making them worse, in fact they were sick with worry and concern. The night was bleak and cold and the snow was starting to lie. But no one even attempted to go home and any one that did, just started gazing into the fire nonchalantly, these were loyal miners wives who wanted their husbands and if they couldn't have them alive, then they wanted their bodies to care for, families had done this for centuries before them, and they would not rest until this happened, then they would go home taking their husbands and sons with them, such was coal miners wives & mothers. Three wives lived very close to each other and no doubt took a little comfort that they were all in the same boat. No doubt the three of them were now widows.

One night about midnight there was a knock of one of their doors, it was a man dressed all in black, he said that he had walked from Bishop Auckland to pay his respects to the people as well as trying to comfort them, at Bishop Auckland the stranger was a local preacher, he was also aware that the poor ladies had not slept for hours. He read the woman verses from the scriptures and they were indeed comforting for the woman folk. In the morning around dawn he was given tea and bread and butter then started off again towards Bishop Auckland, his small deed done in his way hoping he may have been of some comfort to the unfortunate women, some of the verses, which he read to the woman, were as follows:

Let not your heart be troubled
Ye believe in god, believe also in me,
In my father's house, are my mansions?
If it were not so, I would have told you,
I go to prepare a place for you,

For a time the preacher was distracted by men's voices out side, for this was an unsleeping village he paused then continued on.

And if I go to prepare a place for you,
I will come to you again to receive you onto myself,
That where I am, there may you be also,
Jesus sayeth, I am the way the truth and the light,
No man cometh onto the father, except through me,
I will not leave you comfortless, I will come to you,

*Peace I leave with you, my peace I give onto you,
Let not your heart be troubled, neither let it be afraid,*
Before he could finish the verse an incident took place at the pit head, a man commenced shouting cruelly "All of the men are safe," the sleepy eyed people were alerted, by this untruth madly shouted out, all had false hopes, which were cruelly and quickly dashed at a stroke

About midday Wednesday 22nd. They broke a small hole through the debris and then entered the furnace drift leading to the Yard Seam, about the entrance to the drift another crisis was apparent, in that gas was still lingering in the area, in fact the gas was so strong they dare not enter into the drift. One of the sinkers bravely pushed a way through after the gas had cleared a little, George Emerson, also pushed his way through the hole in the debris, described later by him he said that in the pit there was a deathly silence not a sound of anything welcomed him. He found some tools later identified as tools owned by the back shift over man, and it appeared that they had been trying to clear part of the blockage from this end. Emerson at that time found that he was beginning to be affected by the gas so he decided to go back, until such time he recovered, he dragged himself back where his mates were anxiously waiting for him. The two men who had been working on the bottom side of the shaft were later described as the deputy over man John Sharpe and Thomas Ternant. By now other sinkers were relieving the sinkers and volunteers who would further progress Emerson's efforts in the previous shift. The person relieving him was a volunteer called Bill Adams nicknamed London Will, he was determined to push on into the yard seam and did just that, he was accompanied by two more miners namely Robert Wilson and Thomas Cousins, he re-entered the hole leading to the yard seam and he was followed by his mates and the scenes that met them were no less than a nightmare. They were determined to push on into the pit at this time.

The shifts at the pit had been just changing and that meant there had been double the men in the pit at that time, the men found bodies everywhere. The men passed on through the air doors and crawled towards the furnace where they found their first two bodies who were badly burnt, these in their attempts to get over the furnace and been badly burnt in the process. The men went quickly on towards the Yard Seam where they found more bodies; these were laid all over the place. Walking further they came across other bodies yet not one spark of life were there among them. The sight was devastating, they came across more dead, men and boy's fathers were gently holding their sons, obviously helping them through their final minutes, some with vivid expressions on their faces some smiling as if having a final visitation, some also with a frightened look on their faces, but all at this time finally at peace with the world and them selves, the smell was overwhelming. The medical doctors and advisers made sure that there was plenty of chloride of lime put down to slow down the decomposing of the bodies.

The discovery of the bodies travelled fast and news of the discovery was past on to the grieving miners wives and families at the pit head, there were plenty of painful scenes, at last the long cherished hopes had gone forever, words could not describe the pain of those woman and family on hearing the final news. Further viewers went down to witness the horrible sights that the sinkers had come across, "Oh my canny fellows" said Mr. Humble when first seeing the bodies. They were waiting for the help, which never came, side-by-side, tiny pit boys clinging to their fathers. It was noted that the pit pony corn bins were empty, and some corn was found in the pockets of some of the men.

During that day a telegram was received from Queen Victoria, she was anxious to know if there was any hope of saving any of the poor men that were entombed. For them her heart bleeds. Mr. Carr sent the following reply, 'There are still faint hopes of saving a few of the men from the pit that was dispatched in the afternoon, and in the evening it was necessary to send a further one, saying that all of the men were found dead, with no further hope of any men being found alive. The crowd at the pithead were distraught with anguish and worry over the fate of their loved one's. The majority in the crowd were long suffering and had went without food and sleep for days, "bring out the dead" they cried, they wanted the sinkers to go immediately and bring to the surface over 200 dead men and boys, out of a pit shaft which was not safe and full of gas, the crowd were being unreasonable in their anguish, Coulson and his men had drove themselves to the extremes and taken many risks to get to the men, and now the crowd were being extremely unreasonably even knowing the full facts. Militant elements in the crowd did not even give the sinkers any considerations at all one man shouting "Shoot Coulson", threatening to take matters into their own hands. One man who had lost four sons in the tragic accident jumped onto the platform and if he had not been restrained he would have thrown himself down the shaft. Mr. Coulson addressed the people once and for all saying that if they continued with this kind of behavior he would have no option but to withdraw all of his men, and he went on to say how deeply hurt he was because of this disturbance.

The crowd finally came to order when Robert Turnbull a pitman from Cowpen spoke to them, he spoke in a firm and kindly manner impressing to them that they must be calm and that the dead would be returned to them as soon as possible, he also assured them that the coffins would not be screwed down until each body in turn was identified; the crowd had other ideas in that a twelve-man committee would be formed to carry out this task so that no mistakes would be made. Then a final meeting was arranged in that a committee would also be formed to start a relief fund, and the men on it, would call at every house to get the full extent of each family problem and loss. Later it was declared that there were 406 dependants. There were also further meetings throughout Tyne Side with relief in mind, and in fact by February 19th 1862 there was an amount of £16,000 collected for the sole purpose of the relief of dead miners dependants, after this tragic accident. It was also worth noting that there were only 25 male population left in Hartley. The coffins were scheduled to be buried at Cramlington.

A very sympathetic Queen Victoria sent the following letter ~~

To Charles Carr, Esq.
Hartley Colliery,
Newcastle upon Tyne.
Osborne, January 23rd. 1862
Sir,

The queen in the midst of her own overwhelming grief, has taken the deepest interest in the dreadful accident at Hartley, and up to the last had hoped at least a considerable number of the poor people might have been recovered. The appalling news since received has affected the queen very much. Her majesty commands me to say that her tenderest sympathy is with the poor widows and mothers and that her own misery makes her feel the more for them. Her majesty hopes that everything will be done, as far as possible to alleviate their distress, and her majesty will feel a sad satisfaction in assisting in such measures. Pray let me know what is doing. I have the honour to be, Sir,

  Your Obedient Servant,
C.B. PHIPPS

Dead Brought Out

For a day and a night the sinkers toiled to bring the dead miners back out of that horror pit and to their love ones. As each body was hauled up the shaft a sinker had to ride with it to prevent it from hitting the side of the shaft on the way to the surface. As the hours wore on the sinkers became more and more weary. As the bodies arrived at the surface it was identified then delivered to the house of the bereaved to care for, any body not identified was gently laid in the Primitive Methodist Chapel until such times as it could be claimed by loved ones.

Finally all of the dead were brought from the pit, two of the last out were The back shift over man Mr. Amour and his son who were found together near to the staple leading to the Low Main Seam, which would have been nearer to the rescuers if it had been possible to get the miners out. Being a very conscientious man he had waited until all of the men were into the low Main before he and his son had gone. The men had at last been released from this wet and damp hell into the arms of their loved ones to be cared for, the last time, their job in this life had been abruptly snuffed out.

Funeral;

It was a bright and beautiful Sabbath morning 26th. January 1862, this Sunday was very different to any other Sunday that was ever held at Hartley this day. This was the second Sunday morning after the terrible disaster. At every window white closed curtains told people that this particular family were mourning the death of a loved one, and on this particular day this was the case of nearly everyone in the village.

This would be a day which would relate regrettable historical happenings to the turbulence of the present day, when among the families there would be overwhelming emotion, because of memories now in the past. These were two hundred really good men who had lost their lives and disappeared under the heel of industry, men who had toiled all of their lives in hazardous conditions in order to make a very small living for themselves and families. Now they had lost everything, what a sad day for everyone at Hartley that Sunday not only for their families, but also for the Pit Owners, Governments and Heads of State; and in a later chapter it will be found that these men were sold short because of greed and the one shaft system in this country. One good thing that came out of the disaster was legislation leading to the banning of one shaft mines in this country, and so preventing this horrible incident ever occurring again in this country. But what a sad day this was at Hartley this Sabbath day; this will be the day when the whole country mourns, the funeral procession was four miles long.

Nine of the coffins were scheduled to be buried at Cramlington and it was necessary for these to leave well in advance of the main funeral. Most of the others were due to be buried at Earsdon, while a few would be buried at Cowpen and Seghill. Rev Dr.Bruce of Newcastle held a service near the mineshaft; thousands attended the service and listened attentively to the readings and the Hymns. What a wonderful sight with the backdrop of the pithead, and the wheels of the shaft in the background. The funeral was described by the French author of that time Simenon (*Quote*) in his book 'Mines and Miners', 1868 as '*never before was there such a Mournful Procession even in war time, or Pestilence*', as near as reports could describe the funeral, 'it was 'Incredibly Agonizing'.

Between noon and one o clock a convoy of common carts each with straw covered floors arrived at Hartley and one stopped at just about every house, in some cases a one-horse hearse could be seen. Friends and relations were all dressed in Sunday black to pay their respects. Hymns were sang mostly by The Primitive Methodists who at that time represented a fair majority of the people in those days. After a while the singing ceased and the coffins were screwed down, and the carts were loaded with the coffins, which would take them to the churchyard. The most heartbreaking sight at this time was the little family, which had seven dead.

What a strange procession of death this was, each coffin being followed by any family and friends, of that person. These were some of the finest men in the North of England who were being buried this day, all having the misfortune of being down that horrible pit. The long procession finally completed the four miles and arrived at Earsdon Church Yard, where the miners were finally laid to rest. The gravediggers had toiled in order that the graves were completed in time, fifty men had toiled all day and all night by lanterns to complete the task, on that cold day in January in 1862. One of the graves being for 33 bodies, these were the unknown dead, what a sad, sad, day. This was the day that over 200 men were laid to rest and were now at peace with the world and themselves. ~~~

The Inquest;
The inquest of the miners was held on 24 June 1862. Many of the people connected to Hartley were questioned among them were the following. Mr. Joseph Humble (Resident Viewer), Mr. John Short (Engine Wright of the

Troubled Collieries

Colliery) William Adams (first to find the men), John Taylor (coal owner & viewer) he represented Lord Hastings who was the landowner. Mr. J. Kenyon Blackwell submitted to the home secretary, and Mr. Blackwell had been specially commissioned by the Home Secretary to assist the coroner. Of all of the evidence the most important at that time must have been Mr. William Coulson's evidence and the questions and answers given made a mockery of the one shaft systems in England at that time, and for a very meager amount of money, extra shafts and safety staples could have been installed to ensure that there were more ways out of the pit. ~~~

    Mr., Blackwell asked Mr. Humble what it would have cost to put a staple into the Yard Seam leading to the High Main the vital missing link which undoubtedly would have allowed the men to get out of the pit. Mr. Humble could not answer this so Mr Coulson had to be called to give this evidence. Coulson proceeded as follows: ~~~

Blackwell: What would have been the cost of a five-foot staple from the Yard seam to the High Main seam?
Coulson: *£300 at the outside. Coulson went on to say that it would have taken fifteen weeks to complete.*
Blackwell: then asked what it actually cost to sink Hartley pit from Bank to sump.
Coulson: *The Hartley pit, the present pit, cost 3600 pounds to begin with.*
Blackwell: The Pit shaft.
Coulson: *Yes, the Hartley pit, one hundred fathoms to the sump.*

The inquest drew to a close after mine engineers and also Mr. Humble on the general running of this pit, was questioned. A few points which the inquest brought to mind was that if a little more money had been spent at the pit on a staple, or even an extra shaft, these death's would have been avoided. A further three hundred pounds would have certainly made the difference that was needed at that time, and this would have saved the men's lives. Blackwell further questioned Coulson later in the hearing and it proceeded as follows:

Mr. Blackwell: What proportion of the numerous winnings that you have sank, are with single shafts?
Coulson: *A great number, sir. I could not enumerate them exactly, but I fancy something like 20 out of 84.*

At least some mine owners at the time felt that it was important that there should be two shafts. In fact 64 pits out of 84 thought it was a safe and a good investment for the money. It was also thought advisable that in future that the material used for colliery engines should be made out of malleable Iron, instead of cast metal. On the fourth day the verdict of the jury was given and it is as follows:

Hartley Colliery Accident

Verdict of The jury at the inquest held on John Gallagher the sixth day of February 1862. We the coroner and jury, do find, that the said John Gallagher, on the 22 of January last was found dead in the workings of new Hartley Colliery, having died therein from the inhalation of gas, being shut up in the Yard Seam of the said colliery on the 16th. day of the said month, when the shaft was closed due to accidental breaking of the engine beam, which with other materials, fell into the working shaft of the pit, and there being no exit there from, all access to the deceased was cut off, and he perished from the cause above mentioned.

The jury cannot close this painful inquiry without expressing their strong opinion of the imperative necessity that all working collieries should have at least a second shaft or outlet, to afford the workmen the means of escape, should any obstruction take place, as occurred at The New Hartley Pit; and that in future, the beams of the colliery engines should be made of malleable iron, instead of cast metal. They also take occasion to notice with admiration the heroic courage of the sinkers, viewers and others, who, at the risk of their own lives, for so many nights and days devoted their best skill and energy to rescue the unfortunate men who were lost, and everything which human agency could accomplish was done towards the humane object.

I certify the above to be a true copy.

(Signed) Stephen Reed, Coroner. (Seal)

After much campaigning by miners and press and also I am afraid some further accidents on the 7th. August 1862 an amendment was made law to

An Act to Amend The Law Relating To Coal Mines

7th. August 1862
(25 and 26 Vict. Cap. 79)
The act related to coal and ironstone mines and provided that after passing of the act it was unlawful for the owner of a new mine, and, after the 1st. of January, 1865, unlawful for the owner of an existing mine (i.e. existing at the time of the act came into force) to employ persons in such a mine unless

there were at least two shafts or outlets separated by natural Strata not less than 10 feet in breadth. The shafts had to provide distinct means of ingress and egress to persons employed in the mine. This special act was consolidated in the coalmines regulation act of 1872.

Coulson's involvement in the Hartley Colliery was just about ended at this point, he had still much work to do in the coal fields of the North of England, and indeed abroad in his heart at this time, after this tragedy, he hoped that the law would allow the changes in the present system of One shaft system, to the two shaft system, and also to the material used for making the engine beam. As the amendment above shows this indeed became law.

The final episode in this sad story was the presentation of tributes for the brave men who tried to get the unfortunate men out of that pit and this took place on Tuesday, 20th. May 1862 at Newcastle. There had been many tributes paid to the brave sinkers who attempted to rescue the trapped miners and now this presentation was made real, in the form of medals and money. Mr. Wyon of the mint designed the medals the medals were struck in silver with the exception of William Coulson's, which was struck in gold.

William Coulson never attended the Presentation Evening; he was on the Continent at the time having had a pre-arranged appointment. His son William collected his Gold Medal on his behalf. William Coulson Lived long enough to see the above law come into force. Coulson died Monday 12th. June 1865 five month after the act became law banning one shaft Collieries; and the steel quality for making 'Engine Beams'. In this Country:

Comments~~

When I decided to include the Hartley Colliery disaster in this book, I read everything I could lay my hands on in order to get at the complete facts and any new facts which had not being covered by other authors also writing on this disaster, I read through Baron Duckham's version, this along with John E. McCutcheon's version; he always said that writers on mining disasters always avoided writing on Hartley, for some unknown reason. And also The Personal Narrative of The Appalling Catastrophe, At New Hartley Pit, this was very accurately written, together with 'The Memoir Of The Hartley Colliery Accident'. By T. Wemyss Reid; which had a dedication to The Most Noble Algernon, Duke of Northumberland K.G., who wrote the Narrative, this was written in conjunction with the Newcastle Daily Journal, as a benefit for the relief fund. The Memoir of the

Troubled Collieries

Hartley Colliery Accident was prepared by the request of the General Committee of the relief fund. This was excellently edited and very attractively finished as a book in black leather by T.E Forester also for the relief of the miner's dependants.

All of the reports I have read report on the disaster in many ways like a diary. I have tried to write my book, more as a story, and with as much feeling as possible. I have included this story as it is a big part of William Coulson's life, and shows the very courageous characters of not only Coulson but also his men and everyone else who were involved in the rescue attempts in this terrible disaster.

Some extra facts that came to mind were the following~~

- ♦ Dr. Davison on touring the village found that most of the people living at New Hartley at the time were on the verge of starvation, in that they were just not eating, after reporting this to others connected with the colliery, food was made available

- ♦ Mr. Emerson, Coulson's intrepid assistant laboured continuously, from Friday morning until Monday evening without any sleep and little food.

- ♦ Mr. Coulson of Durham the celebrated Master Sinker laboured alongside his men for most of the time, and his expertise progressed the 'shaft sinking' very quickly. On the arrival of Matthias Dunn Esq. (Government Inspector of Mines) Coulson was still down the shaft below. Although now an old man he was seemingly determined to stand by his post to the last. He went down early on the day that Mr. Dunn arrived and ever since was actively supervising all the work as it went on, and under his valuable direction everything possible was effected

- ♦ Ambulances, hot tea blankets and Brandy in abundance awaited the release of the trapped men.

- ♦ It was noted that on the outset 3 small engines were used, in clearing the shaft and finally bringing the bodies to the surface these were called, the gin, the crab, and the jack.

- ♦ During Saturday and Sunday Jowling was heard from the entombed miners, the metal pipes in the shaft were also being struck, noise was also heard from the furnace area at the bottom of the shaft where men were trying to clear the shaft from there. Alas from Monday morning nothing more was heard.

♦ Fires could be seen all round the pit area, at the time it was very cold indeed, 20,000 people used the Blythe & Tyne railroad to visit the area, it was also noted that every cottage with a miner down the pit at that time, all had clean linen on the beds and the tables laid waiting for their loved ones to return.

Hartley Colliery was one of the oldest pits in the district of Northumberland, near Seaton Sluice, and it was a royalty of Lord Hastings, in 1846 there were problems with water (sea). Sunk to Low Main 29th. May 1846 at this time owned by Messer's Jobling Carr & Co. shortly after this date it was transferred to Messer's Carr Bros & Co. & remained in their ownership.

As at September 16th. 1867 the relief fund stood at £ 46,381,14 for the sole use of the dependants of the trapped miners.

Troubled Collieries

The Half of the broken beam that remained in the Engine House; below the Cage that on the day of the disaster conveyed eight men to the surface. Three were saved from the mangled wreck Later in the Century the type of steel to manufacture Engine Beams were changed making sure this tradgedy would never happen again, two shafts were also required at every Colliery:

Troubled Collieries

The beautiful Memorial to the dead at **<u>Hartley</u>** *at Earsdon Church Yard:*

Troubled Collieries

Sad Burial At *Earsdon*

Troubled Collieries

General view of **Hartley**; *below bringing the bodies to bank a sinker rode with each one to make sure it reached the surface safely. The sinkers were finally exhausted:*

Troubled Collieries

<u>William Coulson</u> *and his men at Hartley pit top, this is the disaster that made Queen Victoria weep:*

Troubled Collieries

Hartley Colliery, where William Coulson failed to get over 400 entombed miners out of the one shaft mine

The Hartley Medals awarded to the brave sinkers Coulson's was gold the others silver; designed by Mr. Wyon of the mint

BARNSLEY (Royal Oak) 1866

It was a cold Wednesday afternoon in December 1866, and it was announced in Barnsley, that the Oaks had exploded.

This was the culmination of quite a number of incidents that had occurred, over recent years, from a mine that was known to be dusty and hot. The Colliery was owned by Messrs. Firth, Barber and Company and situated on the Manchester Sheffield Railway, which ran a mile south of Barnsley. The Barnsley Oak was the biggest colliery in Yorkshire, having 3 shafts, 2 downcast, and 1 upcast, and the pit was some 285 yards, deep and had approx. 50 miles of galleries. By the year 1866, most of the coal had been taken from the rising seams, and now the work was concentrated on the dipping seams. This was an inclined pit, running approximately east by south. It was always thought to be efficiently managed, and the consultative viewer, at the time was John Thomas Woodhouse, with the resident viewer being the much respected, Edward Mammat.

Although the Colliery was known to be fiery, provision had been made to adequately ventilate, this very large mine by having 3 shafts. Two furnaces side by side fed fresh air of 152,000 cubic feet a minute, and it was a general rule, that nothing but safety lamps should be used. Twelve days prior to the explosion, a complaint had been made by some hewers that the air was not as good as it should be, and this seemed to have been corrected by management and the inspector (C. Morton) was not called in. Later it was thought that if Morton had been brought in the explosions would not have happened. The miners at the Oaks had taken part in a campaign to change the method of payment. From measurement to weight of coal, and having their own check weigh man, to ensure fair play. The Barnsley men had been on strike in 1858, and they were actually locked out in 1860, and by 1864, the miners were determined to get their wages increased, knowing fully well that the Colliery was doing really well, all they wanted was a fair share in these profits. In February the miners came out on strike, the coal owners were intransigent, and this caused the lockout. In May they started evicting men from their tied cottages, men started living in tents, in surrounding fields. This was an official trade union strike and they paid the men 5 shilling's per week, with 8d for each child, the owners continued to work the Colliery, with black leg labour; from Staffordshire, and the surrounding districts. Many families suffered and went hungry. Later men received 10 shilling a week from the miners association, and 1/6d for each child.

On December 17th. 1864, a compromise was agreed with management of the Colliery, but there was a great deal of resentment, and it was the explosion, in exactly two years, that would end it. It was also in April 1866, that the miners Association, would decide to pay the widows of men killed by accident, an amount of 5 shilling weekly, and one shilling each for dependant children. For 113 married woman, and 330 dependant children, this would be a godsend, at the time of the explosion, and not one penny would be be-grudged

First Explosion 12th. December 1866

On this day there was a terrific explosion, heard easily in the area from as far away as 3 miles, clouds of black smoke, rose out of the ground, farmers ploughing fields about 5 mile away, said that the ground which they were ploughing was covered in black coal dust, and soot. At the pit head the cages were examined, and it was discovered that no. 2 cage had been blown away, and the one in no.1 pit, was broken away from the rope, the winding engine had also suffered damage.

The explosion could not of happened at a worse time, people were looking forward to Christmas, and this particular day, was the day in which tools were fixed and prepared. So on this very day there were approx. 370 people all engaged in doing prep work, and what made it worse the Management could not be certain where everyone was. On any ordinary day a record would be made where every person in the Pit was working either by Deputies or the person in charge, a further contributing factor was also because it was Christmas, and attendance was extremely high, to boost wages. The Yorkshire Post, reported 350 lives lost, but this was thought a little high, for the first explosion. At the surface relief workers got to work, they renewed the cage in No. 1 pit, when it was noted that the rope was in poor condition, and it was due to be changed. The viewers were in a dilemma; on if at this point it was wise to change the rope, or to just carry on using the old one. They bravely decided to change the rope, taking into account the work it would have to carry out, over the next few hours. The viewers dreaded descending the shaft to see the obvious carnage and loss of life caused by the blast, they hoped that there had been some less unfortunate men, who had managed to get to the shaft bottom through all of the scythe and smoke, and after-damp. All of the roads and bye roads leading to the pithead were filled with people trying to find out about loved ones. The scene was hard to describe, people coming from all directions, the Chronicle, reported on it saying that *'language was powerless', 'To describe it with justice'.*

Each time the cage came up the shaft the crowd surged forward, in anticipation, thinking of their loved ones, then on recognition their relations claimed the injured miner, and the whole process started again. Many of the men and boys were burnt beyond recognition, some were on the verge of death, and were taken home to die an agonizing death. 70 or 80 men came forward from other collieries as volunteers, but most had to be rejected. The explosion had caused a terrible loss of life. Many heroes came out of the disaster, with flying colours, one such man was Thomas Dyemond, he led a rescue party, which descended about 2 PM, they did not have much hope in finding anyone because on their decent, they had signaled but received no response. To their great surprise they were elated when finding 20 or 30 men huddled together near the foot of the shaft, only six of the total were to recover, from their terrible ordeal, and their burns. No new information could be extracted from these men, only that there had been a terrible explosion.

Deadly afterdamp now hindered rescue workers, getting many of the men out of the pit, 38 charred bodies were found, bodies of who, just a matter of a few hours ago, were full of life and hope for Christmas. Temporary repairs were made to air courses, so that better ventilation could be again restored. The whole area of the explosion resembled a battlefield, boys on duty had died at their posts, drivers laid next to their dead pit ponies, fathers laid embracing their sons, brothers lay with brothers, as if they had singled them out to die with, the sight was heart rendering; a sight that would remain in the hearts and minds of the rescuers until the day they died. Some on the plane were not charred, or burnt, but just seemed to be asleep, obviously suffocated, in a lot of ways a worse death than the quick blast. Deadly 'Afterdamp' lingered on mainly between the miners and the rescuers, and the fact that this could still kill the would be rescuers, seemed to strengthen their resolve, to find more trapped miners. All through these dangerous periods the Barometric pressure remained low, and the ventilation was still a very big problem.

Dyemond and his men struggled on in a greater effort to find any survivors at all, and it was only when the very last chance had slipped away that he again relaxed himself and his men, who were all exhausted. At the funerals time and time again the bravery of the rescuers was highlighted, this was also again evident at all of the inquests. By 5 PM 30 men had been removed from the pit. Some heart breaking facts came to life, one man had just descended the pit a few minutes before the explosion occurred, and no doubt if he had paused for a little or been a little less conscientious, his life would have been spared. Another man Charles Thorley had just left his previous pit and re-started at the Oaks that very day. Others had been very lucky George Cotton and George Ibbotson, had lain too long, that particular morning, and had the day off. William Wards had that morning an appointment in Chesterfield, so had the day off. William Hutchinson and John Houram, came out of the pit 10 minutes early, because they could not progress their work, Smith Bates had came out-bye early in order to attend a funeral, he was hit by the blast while he was dressing, being pounded by missiles nearly knocking him unconscious. Somehow he battled through the 'Chokedamp' to safety; his brother was not so lucky he died by the explosion second tragedy.

During the evening the pit was lit up by the mines own gas lamps, during this period Colonel Cobb, cleared most of the pithead, of people and by-standers. Some of the dead were laid for identification in a hut, near the carpenters shop, the terrible work of bringing the men out of the pit went on. In homes the mothers sisters and wives tended to their dead kin for the last time. That evening another would be hero came to the pit. He was a partner to John Thomas Woodhouse, Parkin Jeffcock, he was assistant viewer. Right from the start Jeffcock intended getting as many men out as humanely possible. He descended the Oaks after being briefed by other officials. Others who went with him were Minto, of Mount Osborne, Agnesmain Colliery, and Smith, steward of Lundill Pit. They started their task of examining the workings of the pit for survivors. They pushed well into the mine. As well as 'after-damp' fears, the rescuers faced up to roof falls, which appeared to be at most of the walkways, in some cases these were completely blocked, with coal or stone, from the force of the explosion. The men progressed further, without the use of breathing apparatus or communications. Early morning Thursday most of the volunteers had been relieved, Jeffcock stayed, he was eventually sent word that others were prepared to take his place, while he had a break. Jeffcock replied that they should concentrate on making sure that the ventilation was adequate in the shaft, as the pit seemed to be further growing hotter. The dawn was breaking at the pithead and people started to again gather, more and more volunteers came forward.

It was around 8am and a rescue party of about 16 men felt a sensation in the airway. William Sugden an Oak deputy in charge of the rescue party said, "she's sucked", Sugden felt that a further explosion was eminent, saying, "oh lad's, we are all done". All of the men rushed to the shaft, and were indeed lucky enough to get out. All but Sugden, who felt it was his duty as an official to stay behind. Another Deputy, Matthew Haig, also noticed the suck, which he felt was a slight ignition of gas, and he too gave the alarm. For these reasons up to 6 cages of men were saved, some cages containing 15 men. Some would be rescuers, did not accept the forewarned danger, and lowered a thermometer, down the shaft. The time was 9am and just at this point the pit once again fired with great violence, for the second time. The men at the top of the shaft were knocked off their feet; the cage in no 1 shaft was catapulted up into the headgear, for the second time, in 24 hours. Everyone was amazed and dumbfounded, not wanting to accept the fact that two explosions had occurred in such a small period of time.

The comment in the Yorkshire Post, was 'the heart sickens' 'strong men cried like children', reported the Barnsley Chronicle. Slowly people began to gain the reality, of the situation in that this had actually happened, others stood still and were stupefied and shocked, not able to come to terms with it. The cage was slowly lowered then again brought back to sight; there was no one in it at all. Two men at the shaft top, looked down the shaft and shouted down; into the murky depth below, no reply was forthcoming; again they shouted, and again no reply. This sealed the fate of the 27 men who were known to be at the vicinity of the bottom of the shaft, on their rescue mission. The men at the top were shattered and disheartened, although knowing in their hearts, none could possibly have survived, this terrible explosion; that fired the cage so far into the air like a catapult. Jeffcock and his would-be rescuers were obviously dead. Guards were posted to keep back the ever growing crowd of people coming to the pit head, in the immediate area, looked like a ploughed field, from all of the people walking towards the area. To make matters worse, it rained throughout the night. Viscount Halifax, Lord Lieutenant of the West Riding, Major Waterhouse, MP, for Pontefract came to offer condolence, later that day a telegram was received from, her Majesty, the Queen, from Windsor Castle. Jeffcock, Smith and Tewart and the others must be now dead. The rain that day made the area of the shaft a sea of mud. J.T. Woodhouse arrived and his sorrow was very apparent, because of Jeffcock. Clergymen gave whatever help they could, to family and friends, the whole area was a vale of tears.

The recovery operations were for a time suspended, and people started to look for answers, on why this horrible catastrophe happened in usually such a safe pit. Many believed that the first explosion was caused by an enormous release of gas, at the time there was blasting in operation, when a new drift was being won, and blasting was being done through stone, this seemed the obvious ignition of the first blast. The reason for the drift was to increase and improve the ventilation, of the area. The person in charge of the operation was William Wilson, who said, just prior to passing away, that the ignition started a split second after the last shot had been fired. It was thought that there may have been a small pocket of gas in the stone being fired by the shot. Prior to operations in the area it was tested and found clear.

An Amazing Survival:
There was a further ignition, around about 7.40 P.M. black smoke rose from No. 2 pit, sparks and flames were clearly seen, coming from within the ground, and rising up the shaft, and it was clear that the pit was really on fire. The explosion had affected the air supply in the pit in a big way, the air current now being sucked down No. 1 shaft and the furnace pit. Smoke and sparks still came up No. 2 shaft, and this continued all night long. Men were posted near to the shaft to report any significant changes, and the Barnsley Fire Brigade were on stand bye in case of any surface fires.

Time passed until Friday morning, 14th. Of December, this was the day when an extra-ordinary happening would take place; the signal bell in No.1 shaft was clearly heard to ring and reports of sounds being heard from below was circulating, this was reported to be heard from about 3 or 4 AM. At first this did not convince any one because everyone thought it impossible to live through the blast and inferno that had occurred. Never-the-less men shouted down the shaft and indeed a bottle of brandy and also water was lowered down by rope to see if there was any response. The rope was again lifted and to every-ones astonishment, the bottles had been taken off the rope. Hope was again revived that someone off the search party was still alive. The men hurriedly got a coal tub, and made it ready for a descent down the shaft, a small steam engine was started to draw anyone in the tub, out from the depth and to safety.

Despite the danger of still further explosions 2 men volunteered to be lowered down into the depth of the unknown. The descent down the shaft was precarious to say the least, pumps had been damaged, and water poured on to them like water falls, and it was impossible to keep their lights working, and all of the time there was a constant worry that the pit would erupt once more. At the bottom of the shaft they found one man, Samuel Brown, there were no other sign of life, everything was strange, and ghost like; broken timber were all over the place, wrecked corves, and timber burnt fiercely and there was no chance of anyone proceeding into the pit more than 20 yards, without running into major problems of falling stone and coal. The explosion had wreaked almighty havoc, throughout the pit. There was nothing to be seen of Parkin Jeffcock and his men; it just appeared that they had been blasted away.

Samuel Brown was one of a party of men who descended on Thursday morning around about 7 AM. Sam had gone down the incline with some of the others, where they found 2 more bodies, after returning to the shaft again they set off in-bye, but came across people rushing towards the shaft, they had obviously felt the suck of air. Jeffcock it had been reported had returned to the workings, from a different direction, searching for survivors. Brown with 3 other people had gone to a place called 'The Lamp Hole', and while they were there the second blast happened; his comrades, Barker, Hoyland, Young, were killed outright. Brown made his way to the shaft, where he signaled on the bell to the surface, then receiving the answer. Later it was found he made his way to No 2 shaft, where there was a fire he then sat down, and just felt as if he could stay there, but he pulled himself together, and struggled in the darkness, to get back to No 1 shaft and the rest is History.

Later when a meeting was held at the 'Royal Commission for accidents' it was said by Sir George Elliott that T. Embleton & J.E. Mammatt both should have Victoria Crosses, for what they did. Later that day viewers attended a meeting at the Kings Head, in Barnsley, when the pit was debated, it was thought futile, to re-examine workings at this stage, as there was a major part, still very much on fire. The viewers, reluctantly decided to exclude the pit from air, and thus putting the fires out, keeping the pumps working to stop the pit from flooding, put a plan forward. From around about 5 A.M. on Saturday 15th. Of December, to 4AM. Tuesday 18th. Of December, there were a further 14 new explosions, at the Oaks. Some of the explosions were slight some were very violent. It was very apparent that filling in the shafts were very urgent and necessary, and it was started without any further delay. On the 17th. December the furnace shaft was filled in, then the No 1. Shaft was filled in. On 7-9 January, a scaffold was constructed and lowered down the No. 2 shaft; clay was tipped on it with a large diameter pipe allowing gas to escape, and also to monitor readings from out of the pit, such as barometer and temperature. Readings were taken from 30th. of January to 5th. of November, and after this date they started to again re-claim the pit. Before this date, the inquest had been held; there were also meetings to promote finance for the bereaved. HM Inspectors also put a report forward. C. Morton (district Inspector) resigned prior to the report. (A further victim of the Oaks). His colleague Joseph Dickinson compiled the report.

The main questioning at the hearing, centered on the work being carried out at the stone drift area. Neither Mammatt or Tewart, had found gas in the area, the men who were working there were also instructed to check for gas regularly, as the work progressed. Just below the incline where the drift entered the steps, the main south air return, passed underneath, and it was conceivable that the last shot fired, in the drift, acted as on the air return. Dixon showed in his report that there was enough firedamp, present to produce a lethal mixture, which could have been ignited. The explosion came at the time of the day when the forward workings, had been producing for many hours, and there could have been firedamp released from here.

The Barometer readings were falling rather fast, and it was also noted that the furnace fire had been allowed to die down so as to clean it out. It was also very importantly noted that over this period mid December 1866, the fall in pressure had effected other pits in the area, and explosions had occurred elsewhere, notably, 'Talk of the Hill', Colliery Staffordshire where 91 people had lost there lives. This happened at the time of the second explosion at the Oaks. So this pointed to a generality in the presence of Firedamp gas. As for the ignition, safety lamps at the Oaks were ruled out, as the Oaks was well managed, and all lamps rigorously, checked. Open gas lamps were apparent in 2 places in the pit. 150 yards along the old south level, and also 400 yards down the engine plane, both were ventilated by fresh air. The only other open light permitted, was 'Thompson's Box Hole', an office where safety lamps were re-lit, and this was also well ventilated. Dickinson had a theory that it was a combination of the open lamps, and the shot fired in the stone drift that caused the ignition. It was also noted that the last charge in the drift was larger than the other charges, and this particular blast blew into the steps, not back into the drift as the previous one's did. It was generally thought that this final charge was devastating, and it may have been powerful enough to trigger gas either in the goaf, or a pocket of firedamp, in an old slit, or cut out in the south side. It was never suggested any lowering of standards of Management, except that the system worked at the colliery seemed suspect, in that gas from the goaf was able to drift among the forward working face men.

Sadly 340 men and boys lost there lives, on Wednesday, 12 of December, out of 361, in the pit that day, only 6 survived, 27 were killed, the following morning, 23 being volunteers from other collieries. It was a dreadful loss of life, and the public showed much generosity, and sympathy. The union funds, were very hard hit, this amounted to £2,500, with funeral grants, of £8 payable. The union, on 14th. December made an appeal for public contributions. Private donations were also made, Queen Victoria, offered £200, The Lord Mayor, of London, opened a fund, which quickly reached £10,000, in only a fortnight. With regard to the Oaks Colliery, new labour were recruited, new shafts were sunk, and new and alternative workings were re-commenced. John Edward Mammatt, the much respected viewers, when asked questions at an enquiry, of ' The Royal Commission' , of Accidents, the following were his answers to the questions asked.

Questioner; Are all of the bodies accounted for;
J.M. *There are still 80 not accounted for,*
Questioner; are the men quite reconciled to it;
J.M. *Oh yes we never hear anything about the accident now.*
Questioner; and all of these men are entombed in the pit;
J.M. *We have a different set of men now;*
Questioner; Have you been there often, and was it hard for them to get over the sentimental feeling;
J.M. *For a few months that feeling was there, but it has now died out, we sometimes come across some bones, we did the other day and they were sent to the surface, nobody claimed them, so they were buried. There was*

Troubled Collieries

only a skull and a piece of leg bone:
For all the re-commencement of the Oaks, the Christmas, of 1866, will live in the hearts and minds of the Barnsley People ******

The Hisker Memorial to the brave men who lost their lives at the Oaks Colliery

SEAHAM COLLIERY
1880

The Colliery consisted of the following; 1/ 'Seaton Colliery', known as the 'High Pit', and at the time of sinking was owned by the 'Hetton Coal Company', sank by William Coulson on 31st July 1844; began in Ernest 12th. August 1845. 2/ The 'Low Pit', was owned by the 'Marquis of Londonderry', and was sunk 13th. April 1849; producing coal by 27th. March 1852. By November 1864 Seaton High Pit was sold to the 'Londonderry Family'. This happened to be two years after the Hartley Colliery disaster and after which legislation was changed in that all Collieries now required two shafts; after the entombing of the poor miners there in 1862, when William Coulson could not get them out because the only shaft had been blocked by the massive broken engine beam. Bringing both shafts together made economical sense at Seaham as the shafts were only one hundred and fifty yards apart; the Low being 1797 feet in depth and the High 1819 feet deep. Both bored to a diameter of fourteen feet.

Another reason why it made economical sense was that coastal pits were hard to sink because of water feeders and quick sands. Lessons were learned from the sinking of Murton Colliery a short distance away from Seaham. After only two hundred feet the sinkers there, were confronted by terrible problems concerning water. They finally had to install nine pumping engines a total of 1,584 H.P. to control 10.000 gallons of water a minute they also had to use a unique method of sinking by freezing the water as there were also problems with sea tides; with a final cost being in the region of £250,000 pounds sterling.

From the date of the sinking to the year 1880 there were a total of seven explosions in all. In the year 1852 there were three explosions with a loss of six lives, 1862 two lives lost, 1871 twenty six lives lost, 1872 nil, and finally 1880 when there was a total of 164 lives lost. The first major explosion was Wednesday 25th. October 1871 when twenty-six lives were sadly lost. There is a gravestone at New Seaham Church yard inscribing each of the twenty-six men and boys also included is Thomas Dobson aged thirteen years.

All Newspapers from the area reported on the terrible deaths at the 'Nicky Nack Pit'. It was further reported that the people of Seaham Harbour were fortunate indeed in that the explosion occurred at 11.30 PM. When most of the men and boys were away from the pit. If the explosion had happened in the day shift the result would have been horrific. A crowd began to gather at the Pit Head, after the vibration had been felt in the area. Ventilation doors and brick stopping had been blown out without effort. One of the first causality reports was that of Charles Lawson who had been blown into the shaft sump. There were also reports of ponies dying in their stables, which were situated, 1.5 miles in-bye.

The explosion had coincided with the firing of a shot by back-bye men who were developing a roadway. These were the Hutchinson's, father and son who at this time were widening the roadway at a well-known area called the 'Curve'. This connected the High and Low pit shafts and had originally been put through the stone and created a Curve. There was a coincidence in this area in that three explosions had occurred here; none ever finding the reason why. Later Mr. Hutchinson was cross-questioned on the fact that the explosion was triggered at the exact time of firing the shots.

Part of his testimony was as follows *"my son lit the shot then walked up the bank in-bye" "I walked out-bye down the bank with the powder bottle in my hand, to prevent anyone from coming at the time that the shot was exploded"... "I stood looking at the straw about thirty yards away more or less but out of the way of the shot".... "The shot exploded and the fire came momently – both together" ... "there seemed no destingtion".* Hutchinson could not be moved on this testimony and if any thing it increased his resolve, saying "I am not going to tell a lie for any man on earth". He went on to say. *"I saw the shot go off, and then the fire was on me"... "The two things happened at the same time". "I am quite sure the explosion never came before the shots were fired". "Just as two men might be running and come into collision".* Hutchinson's evidence was constantly discussed around the Seaham area for years. Hutchinson had been the only survivor in that area and had lost his dear son. What Hutchinson senior was not aware of at this time was that in a further nine years he would himself be killed by explosion at the same pit in the year

1880. The inquest was held at the 'New Seaham Inn' where Mr. John Rutherford was Landlord. After three months delay and including two adjournments. The Jury finally gave its verdict, which was the following. "Twenty six men died Accidentally from an explosion caused by an out burst of gas from the roof of Number 2 Bankhead of Number 3 pit". The press critisised the verdict especially when stoppings were quickly Re-installed within the pit, sealing the bodies of most of the dead. By the following Sunday the furnace was re-lit and men returned to work with disregard to some of their dead comrades. One lesson was certainly learned from the explosion in 1871 was that Seaham pit was fiery and known then and thereafter as "Hell Pit".

Seaham Colliery 1880

It was 2.20 A.M. Wednesday 8th. September 1880. Most of Seaham Village slept while 231 men and boys worked hard to complete their shift prior to being relieved by the fore-shift around 3am. The men and boys were 2000 feet below ground, some far out to sea where the seams dipped to an angle lower. Before the caller-up could arouse the fore-shift the pit exploded and everyone rushed to the pithead. Even far out to sea ships had heard the explosion and as far as Murton the earth trembled. A great cloud of dust was blown from both shafts skywards.

Many volunteers came forward but rescue could not be progressed as both shafts were blocked by debris and it was 12 hours before a descent could be made. At this time both cages were idle. Nineteen survivors were saved from the 'Main Coal', from the 'Low Pit', shaft, and it gave people some hope that it was not that serious. But it was thought that the reason was that this seam was not as deep as other seams and the shaft was not blocked here.

The main rescue was actually progressed from the 'High Pit', shaft using a kibble. By this method a further forty-eight men and boys were brought out alive. By midnight on this day sixty-seven had been rescued leaving 164 still missing. There were 181 pit ponies dead; later hooves and shoes were preserved as souvenirs. As the rescue parties pushed into the pit the signs of explosion were heart rendering. Men and ponies were badly mutilated and fires were still burning in some areas and had to be extinguished. Heavy falls of stone were also apparent. Rescuers arriving at, and descending number 3 shaft were drenched with water; some having to rest after exhausting themselves; their places readily filled by volunteers. The Colliery Manager was very apparent working as hard as any, his worried care worn face there for all to see. As time went on less & less survivors were found and straw based carts began to appear for the dead. A house was set up very near to the shaft for the dead bodies. Carpenters toiled all hours making coffins in the joiners shop and stocked close by. Dead bodies were wrapped in flannel and canvas; making sure each had their numbered lamp close by, for further identification when families were not able to identify them. The rescue workers toiled for long hours to recover the bodies, W.N. Atkinson the mines inspector among them. This is the family I have mentioned many times in the stories I have researched, this particular Atkinson wrote a story about his particular experiences while being part of the rescue operation at Seaham. All of the family was infact 'Mines Inspectors'; while I researched Stanley I found that J. B. Atkinson of the same family questioned facts on the cause of Stanley disaster. He even took on the Establishment and questioned the procedures of the Coroner Mr. William Carr. Later at Senghenydd in 1913 Doctor W.N. Atkinson of the same family who at the time was the 'South Wales Divisional Inspector', was involved in the largest Colliery explosion in our history when 400 men and boys lost their lives and also included in my book.

Mr. Atkinson was involved at Seaham when 28 bodies had to be sealed in the Maudling seam, which was on fire and full of after damp gas. He had the very unpleasant job of issuing the certificates when they could eventually be buried after a year; the final body was recovered September 6th. One year after the explosion. Queen Victoria telegraphed the Colliery offering sympathy to the families of the bereaved, Sir William Harcourt at the time Home Secretary came to Seaham. The relief fund soon topped £12,000. The time came for the official enquiry which was due to be held at the 'Londonderry Institute', Seaham; one thing that was very apparent at the time and that was there was a great deal of discontent in the area leading to strikes and many demonstrations.

Enquiry
One thousand five hundred men and boys were employed at the Colliery from which there was an output of coal of half a million tons each year. The seams as already mentioned were 'Main Coal', 'Hutton', and 'Harvey'. As the pit progressed towards the sea the seams dip very gently until the depth of the seams were deeper than the shafts. The explosion happened in the middle level, which included the Hutton and Maudling seams. While in later years giant fans controlled the circulation of air; at the time of the

explosion at Seaham the fresh air entered the workings from the downcast shaft. The air was drawn round, and then out of the pit again via. the up cast shaft helped by a furnace and a high chimney. Seaham like many coastal pits for example Easington were known to be dry and dusty at tests completed around 1868 Seaham was probably the worst tested; it was an explosion waiting to happen (*infact there were seven explosions*) because of this, the content of gas had to be closely monitored.

There were three theories on the cause of the 1880 explosion; from which any one could have caused the ignition.

1/   Fall of stone releasing gas at No. 1 Hutton when gas was released which came in contact with a Clanny Safety Lamp carried by a man named Ramshaw. (*Colliery owners favoured this one*)

2/   Repair men Venners, Hindson, and others who were enlarging refuge holes fired shots into stone.

3/   At the 'Curve', as in 1871 repairmen including a man called Brown were carrying out repair work again enlarging refuge holes near to the notorious 'Curve', where two shafts merged. Again it was stated that the explosion happened in conjunction with the firing of a shot into stone by the repairmen.

The Government Inspectors and miners representatives were of the opinion that Brown's shot at the 'Curve', caused the explosion; while the Jury for some strange reason gave an open verdict as follows '*We have came to the conclusion and are all agreed that an explosion took place causing the death's of James Brown and others at Seaham Colliery on 8th. September. But as to the seat of the explosion we have not been able to determine. As to the other question of the firing of shots and clearing away coal dust we think that it may be left in the hands of the Managers:*

It would appear that the opportunity to correct many problems at Seaham Colliery was wasted. There were obvious coal dust problems and procedure when firing shots needed reviewing.

Later Sir Fredrick Abel (President of the Institute of Chemistry) was called in to investigate the coal dust problem. Mr. Abel stressed the dangers of the areas called the 'Curve', where there was a great deal of dust and where Brown's shot was fired. Later there was also an enquiry on the use of explosive to fire stone and indeed the use of firing shots in general.

Conclusion

There were many sad tales after the explosion some so bad that it became unreal and hard to tell some of the horrific stories at Seaham. Mr.

Troubled Collieries

Huchinson who felt sure that the shot he fired into stone in 1871; did not make it this time and joined his son in death. There were many lives lost at Seaham because of entombment; men who were cut off and where it was impossible to reach safety because of the explosion they left evidence of their final hours Michael Smith scratched a letter for his wife on his water bottle. Knowing his son was very ill his father hoped to be with him in heaven that day (*the little boy died that very same day*)

Mr. Cole, who was entombed at the Colliery, also wrote the following on a board, which was very clear and preserved at 'Seaham Colliery Offices'.

'The Lord has been with us, we are all ready for heaven'

Ric. Cole 2.30 Thursday.

Above the board where Mr. Cole wrote about being in the Presence of Christ at the 'Prayer Meeting', with the Entombed men; below the memorial in Durham Cathedral:

THE MINERS' MEMORIAL IN DURHAM CATHEDRAL

Troubled Collieries

Colliery consisted of the following; below 1/ 'Seaton Colliery', known as the 'High Pit', No. 3 Shaft and at the time of sinking was owned by the 'Hetton Coal Company', sank by William Coulson on 31st July 1844; began in ernest 12th. August 1845. 2/ The 'Low Pit', Number 1 & 2 shafts. above was owned by the 'Marquis of Londonderry', and was sunk 13th. April 1849; producing coal by 27th. March 1852. By November 1864 Seaton High Pit was sold to the 'Londonderry Family' and traded as one Colliery to comply with Legislation:

Troubled Collieries

Above the 'Mill Inn', Seaham, Where the 'North of England Mechanical Engineers', first meetings took place. The Inn was also where the 1852 Explosion Inquest was held, also the site of the Election Riots in 1874, Below 'Seaham Hall', where Byron was married. Lord Londonderry also owned the Hall & gave it to the Seaham people as a Sanatorium:

Troubled Collieries

Would be rescuers, descend the shaft in the kibble after the cages were unable to work; to search for any survivors:

Below the first body arriving to Bank in the kibble:

SENGHENYDD COLLIERY 1913 WALES

*T*he Welsh people have a long history of mining, they have also had their fair share of Disasters. Without doubt; the worst was Senghenydd, in 1913. Wales half way through the 18th. Century produced some 8.5 million tons of coal. As the 18th. Century grew to a close; Wales was producing 56.8 million tons of coal. It was a fact that in 1913, the Coal Industry, in Wales employed approximately, 250,000 people, and the coal produced was very good quality. Shipments from Welsh ports of coal amounted to 37 million tons, being 40% of the total British export total. The sad fact in all this was that most of the pits in Wales were hot and dusty, and therefore gaseous, and there were significantly more explosions in South Wales than any-where else in Great Britain.

The greatest accident in the South Wales Coalfield is without doubt Senghenydd, in 1913, one year before the Great War. This is where 439; men and boys lost their lives. This was the tragedy of all tragedies, and would cause much heartache in the Welsh valleys. The colliery was owned by the 'Lewis Merthyr Consolidated Colliery Group', and had been sank in 1890, and had produced quality coal since 1896. The colliery was at the head of the valley of the Aber, five miles North West, of Caerphilly. Over the years luck had not been on the side of Senghenydd, and beside the major explosion in 1913, there had been smaller incidents. On 24th. May 1901 a terrible explosion occurred which violently killed every man working underground at the time, with the exception of one man. It was thought that coal dust had a lot to do with it, as at the time it was very much part of the atmosphere at the pit, and played an active part in the propagation. The deaths on this occasion were 81. These deaths hardly had any effect on production, as by 1913, the pit was producing 1800 tons daily. All of this period the pit was subjected to high releases of gas, and a further explosion happened in October 1910, after which men were withdrawn. A measurement, of firedamp taken, a month before the major disaster, showed, 1,200 cu feet, was generated per minute.

The colliery had two shafts, the Lancaster, (downcast), and the York, (up cast), both approx. 650 yards deep, there were 3 seams of coal. On the West side the seams were six feet high; six districts were needed to extract this coal. They were West York, Mafeking, Kimberley, Ladysmith, and lastly Botanic. Ventilation was provided by a Walker type, steam driven, fan, which gave off a current of 200,000 cubic foot a minute. The pit was worked mainly by the day shift, which began at 5am. And finished at 2 pm. The pit was examined by firemen who, would go down, about one and a half hours before the shift was destined to start, they would spend 1 ½ hours at this task, prior to the shift starting, baronic pressures were also checked, but these readings were not kept at the pit, and these had shown a significant drop, in the past few days, while all other checks were found quite normal.

The day was Tuesday 14th. Of October; every-one was at the pit as normal, and proceeded to their various jobs. At about 8.10 am. a very large explosion was heard, for miles, around, in one household a little boy said, "Daddy" "Daddy". People made their way to the pithead, where smoke rose high from the shaft. The mine manager, Edward Shaw, was already in the area of the shaft, he ran towards the shaft and found a mass of wreckage, at the top of the Lancaster shaft, and this is where he found the banks-man dead. No one can imagine the thoughts going on in Shaws mind at this time, knowing fully well that he had 900 men in the pit, and the only consolation being that the explosion had not travelled right through the whole pit.

Most of Shaw's decisions had to be taken by him at this time, as all of his main officials were in the pit. Calls went quickly out to rescue brigades, and also fire brigades. Finally contact had to be made with people now underground. There was a lot of delay getting in contact with other rescue services, one in particular, being the 'Porth Rescue Services', who were not contacted until 10 am; there was further delay when their transport had problems. Senghenydd had their own highly trained rescue team but breathing equipment was kept away from the premises, so they were not effective on their own, and had to wait for other rescue teams to be effective. Edward Shaw showed tremendous bravery, when with one of his overman, took the cage at the 'York Pit' and descended as far as he was allowed. This was highly dangerous as this shaft also had been damaged, and the cage jammed at the 6 feet seam, over 500 feet from the surface. The manager shouted the further 100 feet, when all of the return answers came from the east side, proving that this side had escaped much of the explosion, while their comrades on the west side had obviously taken the brunt of it, and it will be these, that had suffered the most from this horrible disaster.

Edward Shaw eventually reached the 'Main West Level', which ran opprox. 2 miles in length, branching off into several districts, and here the mine was badly on fire. Later it was described how they tried to enter the districts, but it was just like walking into a furnace. Shaw instructed Thomas and his party, to go into the east side, and get people organized; then Shaw himself, decided to have another go at the main 'West Side'. This was very brave on his part, as this area was really ablaze, and the dangers they would have to face were enormous especially without the proper equipment. Shaw pushed into the district, he found fiercely burning timber everywhere, smoke and gasses blinded and choked him, and he regrettably found that he had no alternative but to again withdraw. It was later thought that with a specially trained team and equipment they may have been able to save people. On his return Shaw found the 'East Side' progressing, with injured miners being sent to the surface.

They were transported to bank in batches of 28, to a cage; this was done in an orderly fashion, and there was never any sign of panic. All of the miners brought out had genuine thoughts of the less fortunate miners, who would never get out alive. Shaw himself returned to the surface, there was nothing he could do in the absence of the rescue services, and he could progress matters better, from the here. Shaw noticed that the water pipes had been damaged on the way to the surface, and he arranged to get these repaired, without further delay, to get water to the forward areas, of the pit. Later it was thought that if they had a better watering system and the breathing apparatus equipment, had been kept on the premises, more lives would have been saved. Because of all of the calls that had gone out, many mining men were on their way to the pit at that time, among them Colonel Pearson, a mines inspector, who was able to descend the pit within an hour of the actual explosion. Dr. W.N. Atkinson, Inspector, of the South Wales Division, was also on his way. The rescue parties finally arrived, from Crumlin, Aberdare, Rhondda, and Rhymney Valleys. Red Cross people turned up, and dozens of other men offered their services. Colonel Pearson and a set of men attempted to put out the fire, but were hampered by insufficient water supplies, and deadly gasses, and they had to withdraw. That evening the Correspondents, prepared their reports, for their various papers, and it was found that 418 men remained un-accounted for, at night, a sad vigil of mostly woman remained at the pit head, hoping and longing for the recovery of any loved ones. Small remnants, of men were found alive, one young boy, received artificial respiration, to revive him, others were saved from being overcome by after-damp, the sense of death hung heavily over Senghenydd.

On Saturday and Sunday, 18th. & 19th. The burials started to take place, of those already brought out of the pit, and many sad stories started to emerge. All kinds of tales started to come back with the rescuers; all of the time there was a constant fear of after-damp gas. W.J. Rees, guided a group of men out to fresh air, then returned to the danger area, to look for two men, knowing where they would be working; he was discovered the following day dead. Obviously overcome by the after-damp. A final count was taken and no less than 439 men and boys had lost their lives. This was a great tragedy for such a small part of the Country, and the greatest number of deaths than in any other mining disaster in the Coal industry. The disaster left many dependants, mothers without sons, wives without husbands, one such woman mourned 8 men from her house, her husband, 4 sons, and 3 brothers.

Relief Fund:
A relief fund was quickly set up for the relief of dependants, of the miners, King George gave £500 the public were moved by the sheer scale of the disaster, and money came forward easily. By November 207 widows, 436 children, and 50 other dependants, were being supported by the fund. It was paid out at the rate of 10 shillings each adult, and 5 shilling for each child. Reginald McKenna, the Home Secretary, in Asquith's government, visited the pit on the day after the explosion, he promised a searching inquiry; a warrant was issued on December 18th. For a judicial inquiry; this started exactly 9 weeks after the disaster:

The Inquiry:
The inquiry opened at the Law Courts, Cardiff, on 2nd. of June 1914, at 10 am; 52 witnesses were called, and it was found that there had been, several contraventions of the Mines regulations. It was generally thought that the mine was exceptionally dusty, and not much had been done to counteract

the problem, the water sprinklers were not working correctly, dust was not properly removed from places where it should. The mine was supplied with the 'Cambrian Lamp', made by 'Thomas and Williams', while the lamp was approved under sections, 33 of the 1911 act. The lamps in use at Senghenydd, had the wrong type of glass installed, and these were not approved in 1913. The time spent early morning, on checks, were not adequate. There was a practice of testing for high gas, with the aid of a lamp hung on a stick, and this practice was not accurate enough, to see any increase in the flame in determining the percentage of gas present.

One person who did this test regularly said that for some weeks now there had been a high degree of gas present, which had been noted. Ben Thompson (night shift fireman) said that gas had been found in three places, in the Western part of the pit, and Atkinson went on to say that in his opinion the ignition started in the Mafeking District of the pit. The underground fires were all put out and this revealed heavy roof-falls, in the main 'West Level'. The mine manager was of the opinion that these happened prior to the explosion, releasing methane gas and at the same time interfering with the ventilation, the gas could have been ignited by a lamp, or sparks caused by falling rocks.

The inquiry went on and on, and it was not until the eleventh hour, that it was decided to institute proceedings, against the manager and owners, and it seemed somewhat farcical, that the manager was convicted on 5 counts, and fined a total of £24, even with pressure from, The South Wales Miners Federation, who at the time were crying for blood, for their 400 comrades. By now the year was 1915 and thousands of young British men were loosing their lives in battle, in France, and thereafter a further war. But no terrible loss of life, could take away from the Welsh people, the horrible deaths of 400 good men and boys on that terrible long autumn day in 1913.

TUDHOE COLLIERY 1882

By 1873 things changed for the worst in the north of England. Miner's wages were reported throughout the area to have dropped considerably; furnaces and ironworks in the area were feeling the pinch. The Rosedale Furnaces at West Cornforth, which was reported to be the largest in the world, were damped down; many pits closed including Windlestone where the Pease family had spent at least £250,000 closed, because of problems with water. Dean Bridge Colliery, also closed, which employed 1,400 men and boys because of an unfair Royalty rent. The prices of food and flour escalated; these were certainly sad times. Spennymoor being the main market town for the area was affected tremendously by the lack of money; people left in droves, leaving half of the houses unoccupied. Although some, had previously given a commitment to stay in the area by purchasing property; many of the other lending Societies collapsed, having no income from deserted properties.

On Tuesday 18th. April 1882 a terrible explosion occurred at Tudhoe Colliery. This was the third explosion in succession in the north east the first in the sequence starting at Seaham, then Trimdon and now it was Tudhoe; twenty-four hours later came West Stanley. The miners at Tudhoe had been uneasy for some time now, even though the Colliery was reputed to be one of the safest pits in the district. It was strange that an old woman in the area had predicted the explosion would happen within six days; the police who thought that she was a crank questioned her; even so, men left perfectly good jobs at the pit, because of general feelings of tension. The six days came and passed much to the relief of people involved with the Colliery, and they breathed a sigh of relief; a further fourteen days passed then one day a terrible explosion happened at the Colliery when thirty seven men and boys lost their lives. The explosion happened in the

Troubled Collieries

Brockwell seam at number six and Sunderland Bridge way, it was a dreary miserable morning and there was drizzling rain. At 1.30 in the morning there was an earth tremor; ornaments and other things were thrown on to the floor in people's homes, and everyone feared the worst. People rushed to the pithead where a person called Lewins had just arrived at the surface with the horrible news. Officials were informed and shortly after 2 am.

Four men descended the shaft without the manager who lived at Tudhoe and had not yet arrived. The men were John Naisbit, John Taylor, Matthew Elliott and Thomas Thompson. The cage descended first of all smoothly then it slowed down when nearing the Brockwell seam and it was apparent that the guides of the cage was twisted; the cage finally jammed completely, but the men forced the cage within twelve feet of the entrance to the seam where it was hard held. It was decided that a ladder be brought from the surface to climb down the remainder, but one man decided to climb the rest of the way down the guides to the seam, and the rest followed, not before saying a prayer, one of the number would not survive the day. The cage was sent to the surface to get the manager who was called William Johnson the exact name of the manager of West Stanley Colliery.

The men started their perilous journey in bye, where they almost at once met Andrew Sutton who was employed as a brakeman. His leg and arm had been broken and he had sustained other injuries; it was apparent that the force of the explosion had thrown him to the other side of the engine house because when he had regained consciousness, this is where he lay. Sutton was in great pain and was shivering with the cold. The men attended to his injuries and left him in care then they travelled further in bye. Shortly they came upon William Patterson who had apparently just been involved in the Trimdon explosion. He was terribly burnt and just alive, but later he died. Four more men were found unharmed,

George Tindall and Hugh Jones had been working in another area in the west of the pit and were not even aware that there had been an explosion. All available men decided to separate and explore the different districts; arranging to rendezvous at 4 am. For a progress report. At the rendezvous time and place two of their number Naisbit and White were missing. The others pressed on, the fear of afterdamp gas being an obvious danger. Some of the injured men were sent to the surface, where there were now a crowd of some 5,000 people mostly loved one's of men in the mine waiting for news. There were hopes that the explosion had not been as

57

serious as first thought but the mood quickly changed on the arrival of bodies, the fitting shops were converted into a Mortuary. The first bodies that arrived were Michael Cairns and his brother Robert, their father James Cairns was found some days later. At Shieldsfield Way two more bodies were found in a refuge hole, all bruised and burnt; these were Andrew Coldwell, and Joseph Faulkner. Peter Strong was found, he was dead. The group worried more and more about the two that were in their group and had not reported at the time agreed, and Thompson and the others decided to go in the direction; they had gone to try and find them. At around 10 am. the men were found, near to the entrance of the new no 5. Naisbit's heart was still beating but White was dead. Naisbit was rushed to the surface where he was revived; slipping away again then revived fully. He explained how they had been overcome by afterdamp; Naisbit said that he had seen some young boys in No 5 and he had been keen to get them out. Naisbit and White proceeded to enter No. 6 and they were about 700 yards from the shaft; suddenly the afterdamp began to effect them when they tried to retreat, but the gas by then encircled them. They used their final strength to rush away from where they were but White collapsed. Naisebitt tried all he could to revive him to no avail, all of the time saying, "get up Bill", but he replied that he could not. Naisbitt added that he remembered no more until waking up in bed.

  There were no more bodies recovered until later that night, when the majority found was in 'Shieldfield District', which was about a mile from the shaft. Bodies were also found in the northwest district. The men cleared falls of stone and other stopping's caused by the explosion; then they proceeded further; arriving where the ponies were. Out of eighty-three ponies in the pit sixty-eight were killed. In one of the headways Joseph Richards and a young boy Patterson were found alive, there was a dead pony between them. Richards was badly injured and he died on the Thursday. Henry Sloggett was the last body to be recovered that night, then later at 2 am the men found the bodies of William Thompson and James Rhymer, William Lambton, and Robert Artus, all had been killed by afterdamp. At about 10 or 11 am; two other bodies were recovered. Then the searches came upon a sight that touched their very souls; they found the bodies of Joseph Marsh and Thomas Cook; they were clasped in each other's arms, as if comforting each other when lying down to die in the aftermath of the deadly afterdamp. This was all of the dead in the Shieldfield Way; they now went to the Croxdale district. The first bodies found were upsetting to say the least, John Brown and a lad named William Smith were found; the boy was terribly mutilated and charred from head to foot only the soles of his feet escaping. The boy had been caught in the full force of the blast. James Whitter and Thomas Jefferson were found in no. 5, Whitter had his coat over his head as if to stave off the scythe.

On Thursday morning Sunderland Bridge way was opened out, where they found the bodies of three lads Thomas Armstrong, George Stephenson, and John Lawson who were recovered; then followed Jonathan Gair and William Pinkney. Pinkney was very mutilated. Then the following bodies were found, George Bowes, Joseph Mitchell, Thomas Snowden, Matthew Rutter, James Shaw, William Curry, Hugh Armstrong, John Cherry, John Burns, Edward Jones Roberts, John Lambton, and Michael Rivers junior. The father of Michael Rivers was found near to the shaft in an unconscious state later managing to recover. Robert Richardson was found, he was getting on in years, he had many injuries and also had one of his feet blown off, but at least he was still alive. William Urwin with two companions found their way to 'Tudhoe Grange Colliery' and from there safely to the surface. Others saved were J. Mutton, J. G. Wallace, Phillip Dalziel, Thomas Wilson, W. Milburn, D. Eagle, T. Chapman, S. Hockin, W. Hockin, S. Cook, A. Dowdell, C. Dixon, G. Wood, P. Boyle, John Farridge, and George Eddy. E. Edwards, J. Baglin, John Maughan, and J. Blenkinsop.

All of the search parties worked mostly without a break until Saturday when by then all of the dead were with loved ones. On the arrival at bank the bodies were examined by a team of doctors, wrapped in wadding and flannel and placed in temporary coffins, then taken to their homes. Mr. H. Wraith organized this thankless task and for years the people of Tudhoe were grateful to him. Another Company who assisted with no expense spared was 'The Weardale Coal Company', the directors of which worked unremittingly without complaint of cost to try to ease the burden of the bereaved families. The main Church used by the families was the 'Holy Innocent Church', and most were buried there. Later in the week Bishop Lightfoot came to Tudhoe to conduct some of the funerals; when he spoke kind words to the bereaved families; he also asked them to spare a few thoughts to the dead of Stanley Pit, asking them to purge their grief for them also. The Bishop went on to say that although he would try to console the mourners only God could comfort them, saying "Only Gods boundless heart alone is wide enough to comfort them". Tales of heroism came to light at the three pits where the terrible disasters had occurred; men had risked their lives tremendously for their comrades some actually dying in the process. The first man to be committed to the ground was William White; he was fifty-six years of age, and left a wife and family to fend for themselves. It was said that the 'Weardale Company' lost £15,000 because of the explosion when they also gave generously to the bereaved. A cross was erected to the memory of those who had lost their lives at the corner of Tudhoe Lane; but later in 1891 when a Cemetery was formed for the Tudhoe people it was removed to here, it is beautifully sculpered naming all of the dead.

Almost at once an enquiry was held at Tudhoe to determine the cause of this horrible catastrophe; Mr. Arnold Morley, who later was to become 'Post Master General', represented the Government. The Engineer outlined details of the pit 'The Hett Whin Dyke', was mentioned which was a strip of Whinstone that appears to have pushed up in a molten form through a narrow crack in the earth. Evidence can be seen of the existence of this on the surface near the Nicky Knack, where underground at the same point the coal is charred and useless either side of it for some way. It was also explained that the Brockwell seam was worked out and was now goaf. A current of air drawn into the pit by the downcast shaft ventilated the mine; this air is carried to the faces by numerous stopping's that block up the spaces between the pillars, making the air more direct and making sure that the coalfaces were ventilated. The air returned by an alternative route to the up cast shaft; when returned air comes to intake air it crosses this by means of tubes, and these are called 'Air Crossings'. Ponies haul coal tubs from the coalfaces to the main wagon way where they are formed into a set and hauled by rope to the shaft.

The main wagon way was said to be virtually free from gas because of the air current in the area. Officials were asked what in their opinion had caused the explosion, suggestions were given. Morley listening to each in turn. One theory was that the explosion originated from the No. 6 way; in the 'West Pit' when a pocket of gas was set free by a fall of stone which fell on a set of tubs going in bye, this triggered the explosion as a man was riding the set with a naked light. Mining engineers put the theory forward; all of the time Mr. Morley listened intently, one after one the causes of the explosion was put forward.

The most likely one and the cause generally accepted was; a shot had been fired (*hole drilled and powder and gelignite charge ignited electronically by way of a detonator and battery*) in the main intake in the Sunderland Bridge way. This coincided exactly with the timing of the explosion. This was on the western side of the waggonway about sixty yards from the entrance of Shieldfield Way, where there were double doors. The manager wished to enlarge the doorways and two men named Coldwell and Faulkner were seen just prior to the explosion drilling a hole in the roof near the doors. Later the bodies of the two men were found terribly burnt in a refuge hole a short distance from where the shot was fired. It seemed extremely likely that this shot was the start of the chain reaction and they had obviously drilled into a pocket of gas. There was just one doubt regarding this theory and that was the area was near to the main road way and the air would be enough to disperse any gas, or so it was thought. This was discounted in that coal dust even on the main road way was dry and highly explosive and any gas ignited would certainly travel throughout the coal dust in the air.

For years the theory of the coal dust in the air was looked on as an absurdity; but laboratory experiments proved that it was very practical. Modern coalmines all have dust barriers where basic dust (*ground down limestone)* is placed in order to keep coal dust in the air to a minimum; water is also used to keep the dust down. At Tudhoe watering of the dust was carried out on the main roadways, but not much thought was put into settling the coal dust higher up on the supports etc. Men who had lost their lives and had signs of violence and burning were found on the main roadways, the others had been killed by afterdamp. Coal dust is very rarely found near to the coalfaces; but is found in high amounts towards the shaft, having come off the tubs going towards the shaft and to the surface. At the end of the enquiry it was generally thought that the high amount of coal dust throughout the pit contributed a great deal to the explosion; it would take the people of Tudhoe a generation to come to terms with this terrible disaster and loss of life at their Colliery; but in time like Trimdon, Stanley and Easington it would be a sad event in their History. *****

Troubled Collieries

Monument to the dead of Tudhoe Colliery in the First World War. Can be clearly seen as you enter 'York Hill Cemetery' at Tudhoe.
Photograph Author:

Monument dedicated to the dead of the terrible explosion at the Colliery on 18th. April 1882 when 37 men and boys lost their lives. The Author made three attempts to get a photograph of the Monument but on all occasions it did not turn out, until finally being successful.
Photograph Author

Tudhoe St. Charles Catholic Church, many of the dead were catholic and over the years many services have been said in remembrance to the miners. The church has had a remarkable history; at one time the parish was a centre for homeless children. *Photograph Author*

Troubled Collieries

IN MEMORIAM.
LINES ON THE
DREADFUL EXPLOSION
AT
BLACK HORSE COLLIERY,
Which Occurred on the Morning of TUESDAY, APRIL 18th, 1882.

By Edward Boyle, the Royal Rhymer, Spennymoor.

What awful destruction of working-men's lives,
More fatherless children and husbandless wives!
Ere graves at Seaham Harbour and Trimdon are green
Black Horse and West Stanley fresh havoc have seen

There are shipwrecks at sea, accidents upon land,
Catastrophes happen on every hand;
But death in a coal pit 'mid blackest of gloom
Sheds no ray of hope round the doom'd miners' tomb.

The old clock of Durham had chim'd half-past one,
The "call" for the fore-shift had not yet begun;
'Twas then that the Brockwell seam, treach'rous and deep
Sent forth a dread sound which awoke friends to weep.

Self-summoned the foremost to reach the sad scene
Was one who at home but some minutes had been;
In trenches for pensions vain warriors fight
Less dauntless, more worthy, the illfated White.

"Shaft block'd to the rescue!" brave Johnson did cry,
"I'll not as your captain, who'll venture in bye?"
The victim just mentioned and Nesbitt came next,
With whom others followed, prepared for the worst.

Like lightning the news round the neighbourhood flew,
Helpers from a distance there were not a few;
We cannot describe all who played loyal parts,
Their names are engraven upon grateful hearts.

A moment each knelt by the mine now afire,
Invoking that Power which alone can inspire
Faith triumph's o'er perils, Emmanuel near,
Whatever betide there is nothing to fear.

Proud rank was forgotten, none courted applause,
Position seem'd sunk in humanity's cause;
Stock ledgers were shelv'd, alike clerk, man, and master
Display'd a desire to stay the disaster.

The cage while descending impeded was twice,
It stuck near the bottom as if in a vice;
Still, reckless and eager for merciful feats
A band of true overmen slid down the skeats.

Such plight when beheld well might heroes apal
Most wide-spread the ruin and huge the roof-fall;
But no sight could stop those who sought life to save
The maim'd claim'd attention, killed comrades a grave.

Amongst anxious friends were heard outbursts of grief,
Devout prayer was offered, tears brought some relief
Yes, as volunteers, weak with choke-damp, explor'd
The wail of the stricken went up to the Lord.

The fan, though part broken, contin'd the foul air,
Else doubtless the whole would a common fate share
Thus Wallace and Jones, feeling nought of the shock
Kept working, as usual, until four o'clock.

A daughter was "asked" and about to get wed,
Her mother had busy been baking spice bread;
Alas, neither thought that an ominous hearse
Would suddenly come and arrangements reverse,

A father now far off on Canada's shore
May see his lov'd wife, but a lost boy no more;
A widow is left without husband or son
A gold harp in glory poor Bill Thom has won.

"Dear reader, a moral the poet must draw,
The purpose of Time is to honour God's law;
The lease of existence here hangs on a thread,
We, too, shall be number'd ere long with the dead.

"This and former warnings the All-Wise has sent
Demand that the living believe and repent;
'Tis written "All things work together for good"
Let's harken to Jesus and trust in his blood.

The following are the Names and Ages of the 36 Men and Boys known to have perished, viz.:

NAME.	AGE.	NAME.	AGE.	NAME.	AGE.
A. Coldwell	41	John Cherry	46	James Rhymer	38
Robert Cairns	21	Thomas Jefferson	61	T. Shaw	50
Wm. Thom	46	James Whitter	55	Thomas Cook	58
W. Lambton	22	James Cairns	55	Edward Jones	19
Peter Strong	61	Thomas Armstrong	16	William White	56
George Bowes	50	Hugh Armstrong	19	Michael Cairns	24
M. Rutter	59	John Lambton	16	Henry Sloggett	16
J. Gair, sen.	57	John Burns	20	J. Snowdon	50
W. Pinkney	50	George Stephenson	17	Joseph Marsh	59
John Brown	37	J. Faulkner, sen.	53	Robert Artus	46
William Smith	17	Joseph Midgley	62	J. Pattison	19
Michael Rivers	22	W. Curry	62	Edmund Roberts	17

WEST STANLEY COLLIERY 1909

The Burns Pit within the space of forty-four years claimed the lives of 183 men and boys in three separate explosions. The pit was quite rightly called '*The Death Pit*'.

The pit was sunk in 1832 for the Burn's family exactly the same year as a bitter strike in the coal industry; when men were being deported, jailed and evicted because of their refusal or reluctance to accept the unfair contracts in the coal industry which made them no more than slaves. The first sign that West Stanley was an unlucky pit showed in November 1865, when the first explosion occurred; two men lost their lives a twenty one year old coal hewer and a young putter of sixteen. Even as early as this the pit was known to be '*gassy*'. In April 1882 the pit again exploded; thirteen men lost their lives including a man called Coulson who was blasted into the bottom of the shaft, when it took a long time before the body was recovered. It was noted that the Coroner in 1882 was named Graham, it was also noted that the Atkinson brothers were mining inspectors at this time.

The date was February 16th. 1909 at exactly 3.45 pm a muffled bang was heard from the direction of the pit followed by a loud roar. The sounds had come from the 'Burns Colliery', a short time later a sheet of flame shot up the top of the shaft. People began to come into the street and head up a slight rise towards the pit. Woman's enquiries turned to screams as now they quickly moved towards the pit fearing the worst. On arrival at the pithead there was a strange stillness, buildings at the surface all seemed in order, even the shaft although it was noticeable that the pulley wheels were still. No one seemed to know anything; one man had noted that fuses had blown in the generating room; another man who looked like an official said he was prepared to go down the shaft as part of a rescue party. There was no coordination at all; no one seemed to know what action to take.

Troubled Collieries

Someone had sent a message to the 'Louisa Colliery', which was about half a mile away for equipment to clear the shaft. At the time of the 1886 disaster it was mentioned that rescue squads should be organized for any future tragedies, this together with equipment; this had obviously gone unheeded.

One man was clearly missing from the Colliery at this time and this was the manager Mr. J.P. Hall; he had been manager of the Burns pit for ten months but on the day of the explosion he was visiting a colliery at Birtley where he had applied for a post as manager. Birtley was four miles down hill from Stanley and that day he received an urgent telephone call 'Explosion, get back here now', Hall moved as he had never moved before back to Stanley; his mind wandering to what extent the explosion was and he also could not help thinking that just one more week and he would be free of his obligations and out of contract at Stanley; but now an explosion which had occurred an hour ago how serious? He would soon know.

Another leading mining engineer of the day was also summoned to Stanley that day this was Colonel W.C. Blackett; at the time he was feeling under the weather but this jolted his very senses into action. The time by now was 5pm and because the informant had rushed to Sacriston to inform him he was rather excited and incoherent. Gradually he got the full story and the extent of the explosion was now obvious; Blackett quickly got into his carriage and drove straight to Stanley arriving there at 8pm. On arrival he pushed his way through the crowds and quickly checked the shafts; both were solidly blocked and he ordered a check on the volume of air coming from the shafts. The Colonel knew his job; he also ordered two canaries to be brought to him, which would be used when the time came to descend the pit.

Blackett had investigated many explosions; he had a unique way of testing for gas, he stood and breathed in and if he survived he fell to the floor and crawled further forward, then he would again test the air. On one occasion he did this and had to be pulled by his feet from an infected area. After he recovered he doggedly returned to the area. The Colonel had a name for always finding the cause of the explosion; but now at Stanley he was puzzled to say the least, he also felt so helpless. Officials of Stanley sent to Armstrong's works at Newcastle for equipment to go into the pit; Mr. Simmons and his men arrived within thirty minutes but they were never needed. There was also other volunteers from HMS Calliope, which was anchored in the Tyne, and there were also gymnastic performers who at the time were performing at the Theatre Royal, Stanley; all volunteered to go underground. There were other volunteers hardened professional miners who were prepared to dig with their bare hands to get survivors out and one of these men was the authors grandfather William Coulson who had spent his life sinking pits like his father before him. *(William Coulson had to get hold of the cage rope to save himself from falling down the Colliery shaft; later he got blood poisoning in his legs. On his death bed Coulson wrote a 'Monologue', on the Stanley disaster and his granddaughter 'Ida Heslington' recited this at functions throughout the North East).* The words to this were lost after Ida died.

There were many heart breaking stories to come out, Tom Riley, was in the pit he had a wife and eleven children, Luke Reay had a wife and eight children; almost all of the Hodgson's family were in the pit; in one street alone there were only two men that were not. It was a terrible sad day at Stanley, Rev. Watson vicar of Beamish strolled around giving comfort where he could; he later sent a message to Dr. Henry Moule (Bishop of Durham), to come to the area and give what succour that he could. Thousands of family's and friends gathered at the pit head, all waiting for the dreadful inevitable news they felt they would find out, all had hope that their loved ones would be alive. The Rev. Watson knelt down and prayed then his prayers turned to tears as his mind thought of the poor entombed men in the pit and their families waiting anxiously for news, that he knew would be somewhat unfavorable at this time.

Volunteers toiled to clear the blocked shafts, but there was a great deal of confusion; great inspiration came from Ralph Stephenson the Colliery engineer, it was he that at the time of the explosion was in the generating shop and noted a loud bang from the switch board; two of the three fuses had blown and this meant that the power for the underground air current was off. He had ran towards the shafts and saw smoke coming out, quickly gazing at the pulley wheels he noted that they were intact; from the engine room a voice shouted that the cages were stuck. Stephenson took another look at the shaft and noted that the timber on the sides of the shaft had been blown off, on arrival at the shaft he gazed over the edge, where he saw a red like ball of fire, roaring could be heard which was increasing. Stephenson stepped back to warn others but just then it erupted just like a volcano blasting him sideways for some distance. Keeping his eyes on it, it exploded skywards bouncing into the headgear; then it was again sucked back into the bowels of the pit leaving the air again clear.

Stephenson was not at all frightened he ran to the ventilator room to check if the blast had effected the fans and he found that they were indeed working; he checked again with the engine house and found that the cages were still stuck solid, near to the top of the higher workings. Stephenson then ran to the compressor house where there was telephone connections to the seams below; but found other people were also there, where they found only one phone worked, but no answer could be found from the seam. The extra help jolted Stephenson's mind back to reality and a shudder went down his spine when he realised just how near to death he had been.

Every mining engineer, surveyor, manager, owner within ten miles radius turned up at Stanley at this time the press were also there in high numbers. The town's postmaster was having major problems as the press crowded into his office to send telegrams. The head postmaster from Newcastle sent extra people to deal with the emergency. Within twenty four hours the tiny post office handled 35,000 words and 600 telegrams; by Thursday this had risen to 900 telegrams; it was pointed out that the explosion at Stanley happened exactly a year to the day of Trimdon explosion, it was further pointed out that the weather was fine as it was also at Trimdon and how it generally was, when such explosions occur. A telegram arrived from the King, which was addressed, to the Colliery Manager asking him to pass on his heartfelt sympathy to the families of the miners; later a letter came from the queen with similar wording adding that she hoped that there would be survivors.

The manager read both before reading them out to the crowd before joining the other rescuers. There was a change in the weather conditions on the night of the explosion as the hours passed by it became very cold and people waiting at the shaft top gathered their clothes about them for warmth not making a great deal of difference; the cold weather turned to freezing when the area was a mass of silver. Stories of miracle escapes and much bravery were happening below their feet as the cold tired exhausted people stood anxiously waiting for news. In the Townley seam at 123 fathoms sixty three men were dead, The Tilley which was slightly lower, there was eighteen dead, the Busty thirty eight would not see the light of day; the deepest seam of all was the Brockwell at 163 fathoms and there, there was a further forty eight dead.

A quick analysis of the dead was completed and it showed an alarming sixty of the dead were less than twenty years of age. This was not a very well known fact because the figures were vague in that no one was sure how many, or exactly who was in the death pit on that terrible day; later at the inquest questions were asked regarding this and caused much embarrassment for the management. There were some wonderful stories told later, one was about a deputy Mark Henderson who was based in the Tilley seam; he described the blast coming towards him which left the roof caved in, for a while stunning him; after a short period he witnessed a cloud of after-damp coming perilously towards him.

Henderson shook himself to reality and ran before the cloud telling others to do the same until they reached an area where there was fresh air. Thirty-six men were in the group and Henderson collapsed amongst them in the group; three lamps were shared by all of the men and they sat down and wondered about their fate and chances of survival. Some hours later the air started to get tainted and two hewers quickly stood up and rushed towards the shaft, seven others followed [*None were seen alive again*]. Henderson begged the others to stay where they were and on glancing at his watch noted that they had been there eight hours. "They'll come, don't panic", "They'll come", trying to convince himself as well; a voice began to hum, '*Lead Kindly Light*' Bob Harrison a Salvation Army, regular sang it full voice and the others joined in; at that moment little Jimmy Garner [14] laid back quietly and died, his little legs had been crushed by a fall of stone it was hoped he may have been comforted by the Hymn. Henderson decided on a win or lose situation at the time fearing that the air might run out he decided to attempt to get to the shaft for help. Henderson went forward passed the two hewers who lay dead after bolting for freedom, he made three attempts to get through after being forced back; he squeezed over roof falls with an inch to spare, Mark covered his mouth against the foul air and finally made the quarter of a mile to the shaft and the telephone.

All of this time the people waited patiently at the pit head, some without food and frozen, out of their minds with grief; one little girl stood all night crying all of the time, and she would not move; an old miner came to her from out of the crowd stooping towards her height, "what's the matter hinny"? "Come on noo, tell me what's the matter", she replied to the man sobbing uncontrollable "me daddy's Doon there as well as me brothers, and mammy died last year"… "Oh my god", said the woman in the crowd "my god"…Just then the surface telephone rang; like a voice from the dead, Henderson's voice was heard and the crowd went still and quiet. An official got to the telephone first "any one there", he said "Aye" said Henderson "there are twenty six of us left", and "can you get us out"? Twenty-six survivors said the official, and the somber mood for a time changed to one of hope. The rescuers in the shaft were spurred on to greater efforts and huge buckets of stone and jagged metal were hauled to the surface. An enquirer asked how many men were in the pit; Jonas Todd the lamp and token man should have known but having no positive counting system to check just did not know. Hall the Manager told reporters in his opinion there were about a hundred, but in general this was thought incorrect and a nearer estimate was given as two hundred and this was the figure that was reported through the media.

The gallant Henderson arrived back to where the main group of men were, and who had been waiting patiently; Mark told them the good news and a cheer rang out. Henderson took the men in small groups along the route he had taken and he did this five times; every time passing the eighteen dead bodies of the break away men. At the shaft they waited patiently for the rescue and they would be entombment fourteen hours more before they were rescued. After arriving at the surface they breathed in the fresh air; giving them fits of coughing, as their lungs had breathed nothing but foul air for hours. All of the men were extremely thankful for getting out of the death pit safely, thanking god, their rescuers and most of all Mark Henderson.

Countless tales of bravery were coming to light more and more, especially in the Busty seam and the Townley seam; in the latter there had been mass and immediate death without warning, Henry Clark [24], William Smith [15], Ernie Smith [25], John Peart [15], Stephen Wood [39], all had violent deaths; the same could be said of the North Brockwell. The sight for the rescuers were traumatic and it would take the rest of their lives to come to terms with the sights, which they saw; some so gruesome I would not mention in these pages. Twenty-six men were saved from the Tilley, three from the Townley, and one from the Busty. The manager finally gave some figures of the dead as follows, 59, under twenty, 40 between twenty and thirty, 32 between thirty and forty, 19 between forty and fifty, 13 between fifty and sixty, and finally 6 over sixty years of age.

The bodies started to arrive at the surface as if on a conveyor belt, one by one. The French mining engineer, M.Taffanel arrived keen to publicise his findings for posterity; Colonel Blackett, whose early illness was now forgotten as he searched for reasons. The Burns family were underground making sure that they got a first hand report; the coroner

Graham was seen with his goatee beard and Homburg hat, he was highly respected in northern legal circles. Larger than life was Redmayne H.M. chief inspector of mines [who would conduct the inquiry], the district inspector Mr. Donald Bain was also there. The manager Mr. Hall had carried out a tremendous job below ground; then there was Canon Body, who was circulating giving what comfort he could, tears streaming down his cheeks, knowing more heart rendering stories than most.

All of the time carpenters knocked together rough coffins, which were housed in the joiners shop, used also as a hospital, as well as a mortuary. John Wilson MP. was also seen mainly looking for blame and if anyone could find it he would; after periods on death ships, Stanhope quarries, workhouses and the eastern coastal pits where he was union secretary, and now MP. and secretary of the Durham Miners Union. Photographers could be seen, some working for the press, some for personal gain; turning the same into postcards for sale and sending them to other contacts all over the Country.

The first party of rescuers had gone down the shaft with the manager Mr. Hall at 2 AM, Blackett was also there; they pushed into the Townley seam the leading man carrying a cage with a canary as an early warning, one of these men was Frank Keegan. The Townley seam was very depressing to 'say the least', there was nothing but dead bodies all over the shaft, and stables. The stench of death was overwhelming, dead ponies also scattered the area. At that time the Manager received the message regarding the men with Henderson and they decided to go as quickly as possible to where these men were waiting; to make sure they got them quickly out of the pit. Dead men lay all over the place some lying peacefully some obviously dying violently and made the rescuers very distressed.

By Thursday, which was two days after the explosion, the joiners shop was full of dead bodies, waiting identification and moving home for their last journeys; three injured men were laid near the dead because there was no Hospital anywhere near the area. This upset Coroner Graham especially as there was also a problem with rats which could be heard as loved ones came to claim loved ones; one woman too frightened to look actually claimed three different bodies, before picking the correct one, after which the body was loaded on to a hand cart and pushed to his home. Men were posted to keep the rats away but they were in danger themselves because of disease off the men; the doctor advised them to take a strong dose of medicine, which would help counteract the fumes of firedamp, which was given off by the dead. By Saturday 131 bodies had been recovered identified, and claimed by loved ones. Coroner Graham decided on a mass burial scheduled for Saturday. On the particular morning more than 11,000 people arrived by train; others came on bicycles, cars, horse and omnibus. The first funeral was held at 1.15 pm. A final estimate of people who had visited Stanley that day was 200,000 some just having a brief visit; bands marched slowly down the high street, playing Handel's *'Dead March'*. Three communal graves had been dug, one at the Church of England, one at the 'Nonconformist Church', and the last at 'St Joseph's Catholic Church'.

The graveside services carried on for five hours; all kinds of incidents happened, poll bearers fainted, crowds pushed mercilessly, women and wives fainted and were passed back by the crowd, the whole scene was utter confusion; but by 5.30 the last man was laid to rest. Having had some military service the Territorials gathered round and gave him a farewell gun salute. That particular night was cold and a chill went up the very spines of people as the last post was played; it was said that not a sound was heard except that from the bugle, even birds were silent; the bugle was heard a mile away; many tears were shed in Stanley that night.

The Causes of the Explosion

The Atkinson family were respected throughout the north of England, for being fair and thorough with their examinations of explosions and mining disasters; they had devoted a lifetime to the industry and had been involved in the majority in the north of England and other Counties, some of the most famous being Woodhorn, Benwell, Wingate Grange, Washington Glebe, Whitehaven William and Whitehaven Wellington, the latter where 136 lost their lives; but at Stanley they were on the side lines, later they would be very involved in the present inspector's findings. The inspectors concluded that electricity was the main cause of the accident; causing at first a small ignition, which succeeded by a more extensive blast within fifty seconds and this, was projected from seam to seam. The Tilley was in no way involved in the initial ignition. Coal dust was thought, allowed the continuation of the blast.

The Inspectors in their report mentioned the willing helpers, agents and managers, officials and other men from neighbouring collieries who all came forward and offered any help that was needed and under the leadership of experienced mining engineers the work of recovering the bodies and exploring the dangerous and complicated mining areas were carried on uninterrupted until Stanley Colliery staff were able to carry out these tasks unaided. The Inspector's concluded the report by stating that throughout the arduous enquiry, no breach of the coal mines regulations act were brought to light.

The year 1933

After the explosion of 1909 two men had not been accounted for and the Colliery had since closed down. The Derwent Coal Company had taken it over and coal was again streaming off the new conveyors from adequate reserves of quality coal. The new owners began to develop the Busty seam, Bob Chipperton and Ted Burton were hewing in the three foot seam when there was a roof fall; after the dust had settled two badly decomposed bodies were found, they had been there 24 years, their lamps were found nearby. A Deputy was sent for, he was John Parkin; who in turn sent for the Manager who came without delay.

The names of the men were William Chaytor [55] and John Rodgers [57]; they had been working as back bye men (Odd Job Men), usually very experienced men. The men had been due to leave the pit 30 minutes before the explosion but they had agreed to work overtime to get this particular job done. Rodgers was a good Catholic and also gambler, he always carried his money with him and it was thought that he would have £30 in gold, he always carried this money, even down the pit and this was never recovered, it was thought that rats may have carried it away. The pubs in the vicinity of Stanley were buzzing with rumours and chitchat.

Again there had to be an inquest. Charles Blackett, after the report was registered still could not come to terms with the findings. Many of the happenings on that cold day at the pithead puzzled him to say the least. Both shaft doors near the surface had been blown off; he finally admitted defeat and went with the main report of the cause of the explosion. Another fact worried him immensely, all of the inspectors including himself had not been informed of a lamp that had been stationed in the Brockwell seam; it was a large lamp of fourteen inches high, all of the mining engineers thought that its design was against safety practice; the Colonel returned home to Sacriston with his thoughts feeling a little uneasy about the explosion at Stanley.

J.B. Atkinson was known as the great "J.B.", of the northern coalfield, the family had acted as mining inspectors for two generations; and they had certainly made their mark in mining history. At the time of the explosion at Stanley "J. B", was inspector of mines for Newcastle upon

Tyne, and his brother held a similar position; the third brother immigrated to Australia where he was chief inspector. J.B was convinced that he had uncovered the secrets of the Stanley explosion of 1909; this had troubled him and many others for years. For some year's coal owners had tried unsuccessfully to suppress him, especially when he commented about the travel of explosions through coal dust in the air; but J.B. intended to take advantage of the finding of the two bodies at Stanley, and air his views at the inquest. With this in mind he wrote to Mr. Carr the coroner informing him that he had new evidence regarding the explosion, which he wished to make known to the court.

Coroner William Carr hoped that he would dispense quickly with the inquest of the two men found when Stanley Colliery was reopened but when he received Atkinson's letter he knew it would not be as easy as he first thought, Carr was a young man and initially he was finding it hard to replace Coroner Graham, but he was soon to face up to what many Coroners don't face in their entire careers the procedure carried on in what he thought was not very important would be discussed at the highest levels and even the House of Lord's. On the day of the inquest Atkinson crossed over to the desk of the Coroner and put down a document, which was a written statement.

Carr opened the inquest by saying that everything had been fully covered at the 1909 inquest and that the finding of the two men was simply a formality and he wished to conclude the business quickly. Atkinson stood up and he said that he wished to give fresh evidence to the court, which was relevant to the present case as well as the 1909 case. The Coroner ignored him and said that he wished to conclude the business, J.B. Atkinson sat upright in his chair saying again that he wished to give new evidence relevant to the death's of 168 men at the explosion of the Stanley Colliery. He added that the Coroner had no legal right to prevent him giving this evidence. The Coroner looked uneasy in his chair and instructed the press not to report the intervention; Atkinson was now fuming, and stood up again to press home his case. Carr, to save face allowed Atkinson to read out his evidence from his prepared statement. Atkinson carried this out knowing fully in his heart that he would see this out to the bitter end, he started hesitatingly to read his evidence.

"In 1909, after the great explosion at West Stanley, I was underground the following day and examined parts of the Townley, Busty, and Brockwell seams. On July 23rd.and August 1st. 1917, after my

retirement as inspector of mines, I was at the Colliery and on one of those days, went underground. I have studied the evidence given at the first inquest, the joint official report and a paper by M. Taffanel's, a French mining engineer, who was underground at West Stanley for three days, after the explosion.

At the previous inquest two facts bearing on the explosion were not disclosed to the court and are not mentioned in the official report or in Mr. Taffanel's paper.
"These are:

1/ Sections of the shafts exhibited at the previous inquest and reproduced in the official report do not show that those shafts were sunk below the Brockwell Seam to the Victoria Seam.

2/ The landing in the return airway at the Brockwell seam was illuminated by two large so-called safety lamps". "These were the weak links in the chain of an otherwise well managed colliery"

Atkinson now outlined his explosion theory.

"The sequence of events were in my opinion like this. There was a fall of roof in the goaf [worked out area] of the north Brockwell district where the extraction of pillars [coal left in] was going on. This fall liberated fire damp [gas], which was carried forward by the return air current over the large sized safety lamps at the Brockwell landing and was there ignited." "An explosion of firedamp and air took place. The explosion caused a wave of air, which blew open the doors on the surface, which enclosed the top of the shaft and raised clouds of coal dust in the mine an explosion of coal dust, and air immediately followed".

" This devastated the Brockwell, Busty and Townley seams and reached the surface via the other [downcast] shaft about 50 seconds after the first fire damp explosion. It was on the surface at this point that the late Mr. William Indian was slightly burned".

Atkinson went on to say....

"There in a nutshell, was the secret of the Burns pit explosion. It was entirely logical, and all other evidence dovetailed neatly into it. Men had turned down the wicks of their lamps? - They had obviously been aware that firedamp was drifting past them and they took the usual precautions. In the Busty seam near the other shaft the men had received a warning by the huge cloud of dust sent drifting into their workplaces by the first *explosion"*. Everyone in Stanley had been aware that on that terrible day there had been two distinct explosions at the Colliery. The Atkinson theory of the firedamp explosion followed by the coal dust explosion was the perfect answer; this also accounted for the thick layers of 'coked' coal dust found on props and at workplaces. Atkinson again had the answer; his statement had fallen on deaf ears including the coroner, press and finally the jury. Atkinson left the court in a hurry determined to see it out to the bitter end, as he left the court his mind flashed on to the Coroners words "*it will be foolish to reopen the matter after twenty four years*". Atkinson quickly returned home, where he couldn't wait to get started with his protest, which he thought on his evidence was a certainty; he first of all checked out his facts and the details of the lamp in question at the library, where he had uncovered the details of its unreliability, and found all was in order.

From his home in St. George's Terrace, Newcastle, Atkinson campaigned for years for satisfaction and to get justice; one further point kept him going also and that was the lamp, he felt that it may still be in use in an unknown pit and they may not know of its ability to ignite gas. Atkinson began with Stanley MP Mr. J.P. Dickie, the Home Secretary, Sir John Gilmour, Lord Lawson of Beamish. All to no avail, even Lawson said that in his opinion the Home Secretary would never re-open the case. Atkinson wrote to anyone that he thought could help, even the opposition leader; he eventually went to the House of Lords and the famous Lord Joicey, who was known to be out-spoken on behalf of justice for mining communities, all to no avail, it seemed everyone had closed ranks on him. Atkinson did not gain one thing from his campaign, but some good did come out for the Colliery, a strict system of control exists for the number of men that are underground, at any one time this is carried out by the count of lamps taken out; the suggestion regarding a little cottage Hospital came to Fruition, the South Moor & Holmside Colliery Welfare Hospital, was built, it was a beautiful red brick building surrounded by lawns.

Disaster Fund
The Trustees collected a total of £17,000 for the care and maintenance of 65 widows, 107 children and 16 incapable of doing anymore work, because of their injuries. By 1933 16 widows were receiving assistance. Later there was a scandal as a large part was lost because of depreciation, when trustees invested in Hudson's Railway shares. ********

Above **Canon Body** *says words of Comfort at the graveside; below Thousands attended the funerals of the poor miners:*

Troubled Collieries

The colliery's at **Stanley**; *below & the 'The* **Louisa'**, *messages of help were sent and important equipment supplied to help the rescue:*

Troubled Collieries

Above St Andrews Church Stanley, below St. Joseph's Roman Catholic Church Stanley

Troubled Collieries

Frank Keegan; *grandfather of Kevin Keegan who was a mining inspector at the time of the explosion, he played his part in the rescue of 26 men:*

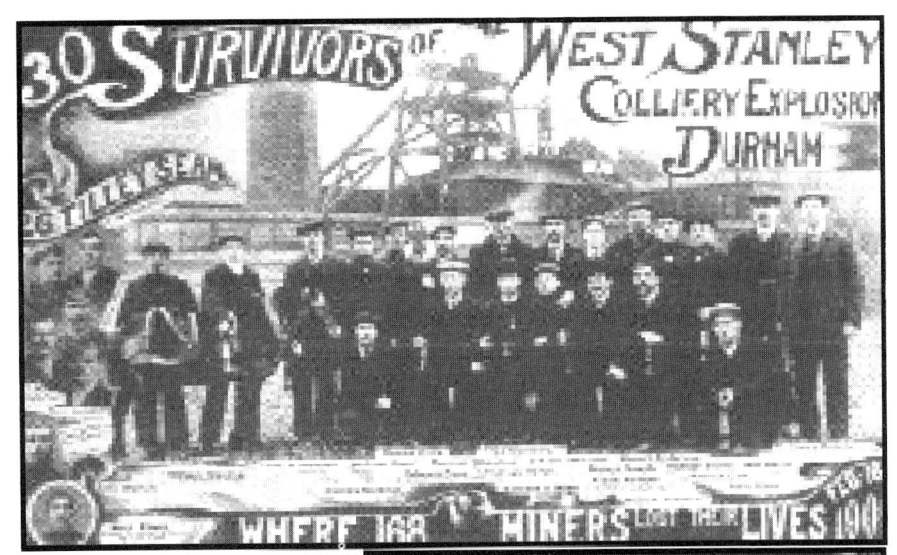

The picture shows the terrific likeness of present day Kevin Keegan the current Manager of 'Manchester City' & one time Manager of Newcastle, Fulham & England's National side. Kevin has readily made himself available for any campaign that has been circulating from Stanley and other Northern Mining areas. Especially with the 'Northern Echo', campaign to find the last resting place of dead Stanley miners from the terrible explosion of 1909. He has also supported me with my other projects especially when writing books on mining areas such as 'Coxhoe'.

80

Troubled Collieries

William Gardner and pony, rescued from the death pit; below crude coffins used initially for the dead until they were identified:

Troubled Collieries

SACRISTON VICTORIA 1903

Sacriston Pit was named after young Queen Victoria, who had claimed the throne of England after the death of her uncle Edward Duke of Kent, in 1837; she was just eighteen years of age. Sacriston Victoria worked coals from seams 'Five Quarter', and 'Main Coal', these coals were found superior enough for the production of iron and also ideal for the making of coke. On the day of its opening it was a grand occasion with many spectators in top hats and officials in Sunday suits accompanied by their wives and children. There was also a railway opening to celebrate and many guests were taken by train to the coal drops at South Shields where they could witness the first coals coming out of the Victoria, and delivered to the "Tyne docks". The route to South Shields started with the climb to the 'Daisy Hill, Engine House' where on arrival a toast was given to the Railway's success. All of the time the band played, and the guests consumed barrels of ale and meat pies. Onwards they went down hill to Waldridge across the fell passing the 'Byron Pit'.

On arrival at Waldridge refreshments were handed out and the band continued playing; a further period of travel brought them to 'Fat Nelly's', Ale House, where further supplies of ale and pies were replenished to last them the final part of the journey, along the Stanhope and Tyne Railway, and so to South Shields and the Tyne and the outlet to the sea. On arrival there were more celebrations with the locals and the return journey was hilarious and the officials and owners and other guests were glad to retire to the 'Lambton Arms', at Chester le Street, where they further celebrated with fine wines and a grand dinner. The merrymaking for the miners carried on back at the Colliery; families were supplied with a lavish meal and served up by Colliery Over Men, while wives and daughters enjoyed dancing and other entertainments. Sacriston over the years was known for its lawlessness, they drank after hours gambled and fought in the streets;

the road through the village was more like a dirt track than a road; houses either side were just like shacks, surrounded by small holdings created by men who used them to grow vegetables for large families.

William Blackett

Around about 1869 William Blackett, lived in the area, he was the son of a local doctor; he visited Sacriston often, when he marveled at the different dialects of the immigrant miners and he enjoyed meeting these strange people living in the Colliery rows 'Cross Streets' were known for being mainly the home of Sacriston's large population of Irish people. The area was known as 'Irish Row', and the houses were in a terrible state of repair, and in most cases not even fit for animals; often Blackett sat on his fathers pony and trap and heard amazing lively jigs played brilliantly on old Galway fiddles. Old Irish woman sat at cottage doorways nonchalantly smoking clay pipes; possing dirty washing with their feet.

The truth of the matter was the whole area was poor and some not able to feed their children; even though rich veins of quality coal lay in the strata waiting to be developed. Now in the year 1839 the new Witton & Victoria which had been sunk along side the old Charlaw Colliery, people had a renewed sense of hope; which was to turn out bad news, when in 1844 fines implemented by coal owners in Sacriston doubled; one hard working hewer spoke of working a full fortnight, and when going to collect his wages he was told that he was due to nothing, as he owed fines; up to that week he was told he still owed four shillings. All came to a horrible conclusion when in 1849, the men went out on strike; only to be turned out of their homes during the winter months mostly in the middle of the night, by paid bullies who were protected by the police. When all they had done was ask for a fair wage for a fair days work.

The Charlaw & Sacriston Coal Company

Around about the turn of the century an element of fairness began to surface at the Victoria and other pits in the area such as Kimblesworth and Nettlesworth, and between them because of treating the men with a little respect and as human beings, produced a half a million tons of coal a year when the pits employed fourteen hundred men.

It was the winter of 1903, and it was a cold November morning, Sacriston was full of back shift men walking towards the pit at the bottom of the village. Two hundred men drew their lamps and waited patiently for the cage that would take them to their various seams and work places. The time by the lamp cabin clock showed just short of 10 am; in the sky there were dark clouds laying low over Heugh Edge and Daisy Hill, most of the men felt a little comfort in going underground, out of the way of the bad weather. Some would not see day light again, some, not for a week and for the remainder, they would have a brush with what could have been a horrible death.

At 11.30 there was a loud bang in the Victoria pit, Busty seam; hewers and putters panicked, dropped their tools and ran, some to their deaths. An inrush of water occurred in the West Board of the second North Flat, which was in the third west district of the Busty seam. The depth of the seam from the surface was one hundred fathoms and one and a quarter miles south west of the shaft. The Busty seam in the area was six feet in thickness and was worked by the board and pillar method; that day many men had very narrow escapes from drowning and some had to wade to safety. When they finally managed to account for people they found that three men and a pony were missing.

The inrush was because water from the Fulforth district which had been unworked, for seven years; burst through a barrier of hitch coal into the lower 'Third West' district, at the bottom of the hitch. This interfered with the coal left in, to divide the two districts; but because of new quarter end caviling (to *make sure good and bad jobs are properly shared each quarter jobs get drawn*), new people were consigned to the area not being familiar with the work near to the hitch. (*A fault in the strata that affected the height of the coal near it*) It was apparent that the area was broken into, causing the inrush of water.

Henry Blackburn was the for shift deputy, he said he was down, in the area of the inrush on the Monday morning about 2.30 am. It was the day before the disaster. On the way in bye (towards *the coal face)* he met Forester the deputy, that was in on the Sunday night and he informed Blackburn that all the areas were secure and in working condition; but as a precaution he checked the districts as well; on the way out he met the incoming men and placed them in their days work. Bobby Whittaker's place was where the water came in, and the following day Jack Whittaker lost his life. At 7.15 am; the deputy had been in the area and Bobby was satisfied that everything was in order.

The day of the Inrush

William Blackett was general manager of Sacriston Colliery, he was also Captain of volunteer infantry, and also a mining engineer; he was also very keen on fox hunting and on that particular morning he was hunting with hounds some where near Cornsay Colliery. This was the area where hardy foxes roamed; a match for any hounds. This was an area where the best poachers in the County learned their trade; but on this particular morning the Captain had not even time to stretch Kitty's legs when a messenger caught up with him and informed him of a serious influx of water at the Colliery, Blackett pulled his mare around and pushed her to extremes as fast as she could gallop, back to Sacriston. She seemed to sense the urgency as the horse covered the nine miles through fields and over hedges in just a half hour; by 2.30 pm. Blackett was underground at the pit.

The Captain met John Noble the manager, and his under study Thomas Green, at the edge of the water; other officials were also there. A short distance away the water was level with the roof; Blackett thought how lucky the men had been to get away from the area, although three were missing, with water on this scale they were lucky that death by drowning had not reached high proportions in the pit that day. Anyone who was cut off would have obvious problems especially with lack of air and he decided there and then not to leave the pit until the men were found alive or dead. Within an hour of arriving the Captain had a powerful pump installed, when it was hoped to reduce the water sufficiently to find the men. A rope pump was also brought in from a neighbouring colliery, but it was still impossible to go very far without putting lives in danger of drowning. An attempt was made to get to the men by the Fulforth district as the water originated from there and it was thought could be passable. Time after time they tried but were beaten back; eventually they reached the district.

The Captain and John Brass waded into the water up to their chests, the slightest ripple sent it above their mouths and the only way forward was to swim; eventually the men found the area where the water had broken in and they decided to make a dam out of props and clay hoping that it would be strong enough to withstand the water as their lives would be in danger; they further hoped that the time gained in this process would give the pumps the time to be effective in the other parts of the pit.

The depth of the water now allowed a little progress and Blackett and his men waded forward; the height of the roof was six feet the present height of the water being around five feet six inches; again they pressed on careful not to swallow the water and as it rose still further it was very frightening. Blackett had his lamp fastened on to his forehead with a belt as he needed both hands to go forward; roof falls were everywhere and these had to be carefully negotiated. By the Thursday night the rescuers had progressed four hundred yards into the area; suddenly Blackett stumbled on a body which as if by magic rose to the surface giving a ghostly appearance on the top of the water it was found to be the body of John Whittaker. John had been found fifty yards from where he had been working, although there was a gash on his cheek and he was covered in pit dust his face was at peace; it was also thought that he had died quickly. The men gently took hold of his body and took him to the shaft bottom and about 7 pm; he was taken to the surface on a stretcher and from there to his home at Elliott Street, where his mother could tend to him; not before breaking down and crying uncontrollably on the sight of her loved one.

The search continued; John Brass collapsed when finding Whittaker; he had had no sleep since Monday and it was now telling on him, especially as he was constantly in the water having no thought for himself. The rescuers were numb with cold and hardly able to keep awake, but the brave men again entered the district; the time was about 3.30 am. On the Friday morning, the men were tired and exhausted and nearly out of their minds with cold and damp and on occasions they nearly accepted defeat. Very near to where the men had found Whittaker, they found the body of Thomas McCormick who was lying face down in the water; again it was thought that his death would have been swift and from the powerful first inrush of the water.

One person was still to be found and that was Robert Richardson; the brave men pushed on through the murky water towards the last position that Richardson had been known to have been working. Blackett was thirty feet in front of the others when he heard a strange thumping noise; many noises had been previously heard and disregarded but this continued as if administered by someone. The Captain excitedly shouted "Hello", and to his amazement a faint "Hello", was heard; Blackett again shouted not quite taking it in what he had heard, "Where are you", "Here", was the reply. In front of Blackett was a canvas door used for ventilation, he quickly opened it and to his amazement found Robert Richardson. Blackett and the others were overjoyed, they shook his hand warmly; all of the efforts in the cold and damp had now been worthwhile and the men were glad.

Blackett sent out for some hot soup which Richardson gladly gulped; saying he had tasted nothing like it in his life and it put energy and warmth back into his cold and weary body. The men insisted that they carry him out to the shaft, and from there he was taken home on a horse and trap. When he reached the surface he breathed the air deeply into his lungs, the fresh air was exhilarating after breathing foul air for so long he quietly thanked god for his release from his watery prison. On arrival at home his wife thought he was a ghost, Doctor Garson insisted that he go directly to bed when as soon as his head hit the pillar he went into a deep sleep.

The following day Richardson woke fresh and well and he talked of the day of the disaster; he was busy hewing coal and there was no sign of the putter coming back; he had enough coal for the rest of his shift so he went to look for the putter and a chumming. Robert never got very far because a short distance away water was nearly up to the roof. He thought about wading through so he removed his clothes but had second thoughts as the water got worse and by now was nearly roofed; he had to accept the fact that he was trapped. He turned a tub on end and laid planks on top, then with his water bottle and what was left of his bait he lay on top of the tub, to await being rescued; which he felt sure would happen and thought that even now they may be trying to get to the area. Richardson glanced at his watch, it showed 2.30 pm. he had now been down, only about four hours and it seemed like a lifetime, he closed his eyes and fell into a much interrupted sleep, he added that the planks were the hardest bed he had ever slept on. He felt sure that he would be rescued and eventually he was; when Blackett finally arrived he said, "You were a long time in coming".

Inquest
The inquest was held on the evening of Friday 20th. November 1903, this was the day that Richardson was rescued from the mine; the Coroner was John Graham who also lived at Sacriston. The preliminary meeting was held at St. Peters Church Institute when John Whittiker's father and also Patrick McCormick, Tommy McCormick's father, who was a wagon way man, gave evidence of identification. The hearing was then adjourned until after the funeral on Wednesday December 9th. When a verdict of accidental death was recorded by drowning, no blame was put on management and mining inspectors endorsed this, when the case was closed.

Burial
Churches and Chapels were overflowing on the day of the funeral; as many as five thousand people packed into Sacriston. The Town band played both funerals to the Church playing "Dead March in Saul"; people forgot their religious differences and were united in prayer. The Mine banner was paraded at each funeral; it was only two years old, and had been seen at two

Troubled Collieries

'Big Meetings', without loss of life and now was draped in black. Two fine polished oak coffins were used for the men and a glass paneled hearse with two black horses; flowers of every description could be seen, and that morning men had collected white Chrysanthemums from the allotments which were as good as the best bought flowers. Finally the men were laid to rest. Six medals were presented at Sacriston Co-op, Hall on April 9th. 1904 they were presented to Simon Tate, John Brass, Henry Blackburn and John Hall; a further fifty gold medals were presented to others for their services when searching for the missing men: ******

Sacriston Colliery new banner on the eve of the 1957 Big Meeting. Dr. Sam Watson unveiled it which shows **'Earl Attlee'**:

Troubled Collieries

An old Photograph of Three members of the rescue team, **John Brass, William Blackett** *and* **William Walker,** *below an early photograph showing the rescuers looking for the men cut off by water:*

FELLING COLLIERY
1812

Felling is in the Parish of Heworth and lies one and a half miles east of Gateshead. The Colliery has been owned by the Brandlings of Gosforth since 1590; the High Main had been worked since 1779, until 19th January 1811, the Low Main was then progressed in October 1810, and fully worked in May 1811. Messrs. 'John, William Brandling, Henderson and Grace' all had quarter shares; they also had a lease from the Dean and Chapter of Durham for the coal which was at the south east of Felling. The down cast shaft was the 'John Pit', which was situated at the north side of the Sunderland road, sunk to a depth of 204 yards; the shaft was used for drawing coals when a steam engine was used. A 'Whim Gin', was used for taking and drawing manpower.

The up cast shaft (air furnace shaft) was named the 'William Pit', and positioned five hundred and fifty yards south west of the 'John Pit', the shaft being sunk 232 yards deep. In the eighteenth century most pits were ventilated and air accelerated by a furnace at the bottom of the up cast shaft; while it is maintained and there are no falls of roof, and the ventilation doors are well positioned, the forward coal faces are well ventilated, but if there was anything wrong with the previously mentioned there was a big danger of 'Firedamp', production.

The date was 25th.May 1812, there was a tremendous explosion at Felling Colliery, which was heard as well as felt in neighbouring villages; two blasts were clearly experienced from the John pit, then a further one from the William pit. The ground around the area for about four miles trembled and vibrated like an earthquake and dust and small coal rose into the air; the village of Heworth was completely covered and the whole area turned to darkness, just as if it was dusk. The heads of both shaft frames were blown off and pulleys blown to pieces, except them that was on the John pit as they were independent; the coal dust which was ejected around the area was three inches thick and it quickly burnt to a cinder; the same was blown up the shaft soaring high in the air and described as not unlike the eruption of the volcano of 'Mount Etna',

Woman and children ran to the colliery in terror crying for husbands, sons, brothers and fathers all tremendously affected by horror, anxiety and most of all, grief. Because the main haulage wheels were not now working, the 'Gin', was put to use; many men took the place of the horses and with the urgency of the situation, their strength was enormous, by twelve o' clock the thirty two survivors were brought to the surface. At the same time two dead boys were brought to the surface, they were scorched and their young bodies shattered; one hundred and twenty one boys and men were in the pit when the disaster happened, eighty seven were in their workplaces, two Waste men, two Deputies, one Overman, one putter, and two Masons, eight people in all came to the surface just prior to the explosion.

Apprehension grew for the people that were still at their workplaces; especially as no more had reached the shaft, and now search parties were being arranged, Mr. Straker, Mr. Anderson, William Haswell, Edward Rogers, John Wilson, Joseph Pearson, Henry Anderson, Michael Menham and Joseph Greener, all descended the John Pit. Because the 'Fire Damp', would have exploded if the men used candles, they progressed into the pit with 'Steel Mills', (small machines which give light by a cylinder rotated against a flint). The men cautiously went forward into the pit, but shortly had to stop using the machines as the firedamp irritated the spark and there was a danger of another explosion, in fact a cloud of the gas floated past them, and it appeared to be ready for the slightest spark to ignite it.

They were in complete darkness and they were choking for the want of air. Finding anyone now seemed remote and there was a good chance of the in-bye workings being on fire; added to this was a high possibility of a further explosion, the men withdrew back to the shaft area where they could once again breath fresh air and where they could check on further ventilation. At two in the afternoon Mr. Straker, and Mr. Anderson, ascended the shaft to check the air problem, in the, 'William Pit', Menham, Greener and Rodgers also ascended; two of the party were still at the bottom. Suddenly there was a further explosion, the men in the shaft, did not experience anything, Haswell and Anderson heard the growl of the pit and both clung on to a pit prop which was acting as a roof support, they faced the shaft and allowed themselves to lift with the blast, and it possibly saved their lives; as soon as possible the pair were brought to the surface, both feeling very fortunate men. Mr. Straker was colliery viewer, Haswell its overman, who had three brothers in the pit; Wilson was a Waste man having three sons in the pit. Pearson had a father and two brothers, Rogers was a Deputy having close relatives in the pit; all having strong reasons to do the best possible to get the men out. Pearson, Rogers and Anderson had escaped from the first explosion, and unselfishly were attempting to find any other survivors. As the searchers reached the surface many people asked for information that they may have on their relatives; every answer was negative, and was corroborated by the second explosion, also pointing to the impure state of the Colliery, and the unselfish attempts by the men. The rescuers did not want to destroy the hope of the people for their loved ones; over the years at other Collieries for example 'Byker', three men had been shut up for forty days and they were found alive; they had survived on Horse beans, and candles. There were many cries of 'murder' from the crowd as atmospheric air was excluded from the mine; to try and extinguish the fires and many women would not go home, they stayed and listened for the slightest sound of their husbands or sons name.

The owners of the mine gave assurances that no expense would be spared to secure the rescue of the men; they contacted anyone who may be helpful, especially viewers, all saying that it would be foolhardy for any more rescue attempts at this stage. The mouth of the John Shaft remained open; while the William pit was covered with planks. On Wednesday 27th. May, Mr. Straker and the Over Man again went down the John pit shaft to check the air in the workings. At the bottom of the shaft a mangled horse lay, they went a further eight yards in-bye, and the sparks from the flint again were agitated by choke damp gas, and Haswell faltered in his steps, affected by the gas and had to be supported by Straker.

They quickly ascended the shaft and breathed in the clear air at the surface to revive them, feeling lucky to be alive; Mr. Anderson and James Turnbull (a hewer at the Colliery) then went down the shaft, Turnbull had been a survivor from the original blast. At thirty fathoms from the bottom the air was found to be very warm; at the shaft bottom they found that they could not breath, having no alternative but to go back to the surface. Their clothes smelt of turpentine made from coal tar; this in some way convinced the people at the shaft top that there was not much hope in finding anyone alive in the pit. Some walked slowly away in deep thoughts of their loved ones, some praying quite loudly, others still not accepting the facts and waited for the least hope at all of finding them. From that time it was resolved to seal the shaft to extinguish the fire and this was done with planks and clay. The officials now went further to make sure that the shafts were properly sealed, more clay and planks were added to the existing seals they knew fully that the fires would not go out until the air was properly stopped, and there was not a great lot anyone could do to help the poor men in the pit now. On the 28th. May, even more clay was added and this led to all of the seal and clay dropping into the shaft; further clay was put on but this too collapsed.

Finally the day came when they attempted to re-open the unfortunate colliery, a brattice was brought to divide the William pit and work commenced to clear the shaft of the clay, and get it back to the surface. About this time rumours began to circulate, not only in the area of the pit but the County and even the Country; that survivors had managed to get to the shaft from the in-bye workings but had then died because of the shafts not being accessible. This greatly upset people waiting at the surface as well as officials and owners who had tried everything to get the men out of the stricken pit; other men in the area also caused friction by spreading more rumours causing terrible distress for the loved one's of the trapped men. On the 19th. June it was found that the water had risen in the William pit to twenty-four feet; sinkers were brought in and a crow hole was bored into the north drift; stoppings were removed away from the John pit and air passed quickly into the mine and out again via the John pit tube.

The officials made checks on the 'Fire-Damp' gas and found that it would not ignite, the checks were made at the John Pit tube. When the shaft was finally exposed to the air the shaft became an up-cast, and with the mixture of air and gas a further explosion occurred; when it was exposed to a candle. On the 7th. July the clay was pierced in the William pit, when a thick volume of vapour, which was gray, black, in colour was observed, on the evening it turned to gray, then the following morning it was hardly visible. On the morning of Wednesday 8th. July it was decided that it was safe enough to enter the workings; a large crowd gathered some to cause mischief, others full of remorse and grief, others just for curiosity. As the air for the areas in the pit was important the crowd was kept back as far as possible, and police constables were placed strategically to do this, there were also two surgeons in attendance.

At six in the morning Mr. Straker and Mr. Anderson and six others descended the William pit, and pushed in towards the Plane Board; a current of water over the past ten hours had been sprayed where they had descended and the air in the airways was found to be cool and easy to breath. The men used the steel-mills, which were now effective; the men came upon many falls of stone, which had to be put right as the circulation of the air was affected. After a while they came to the plane board, where a stopping was fitted to the right, which guided the air along their route to the inner workings.

They began recovering the dead as soon as humanly possible; they used two shifts of four hours on and eight off to do this. The bodies were so badly burnt that even handling them was a task and the men encouraged each other to make the effort. The bodies were put straight into coffins underground and hauled up the shaft by the use of netting; the men used the substance 'Oakum', to put on their hands when they handled the dead. The sight of the dead was beyond explanation, because of the violence and burning. The men were really affected by it; especially on the sight of any one they knew. At the surface the coffins were stacked in the Joiners shop, ready for the next day. One day some coffins were delivered to the Colliery and the woman wailed, howled and cried uncontrollably, there were many heart-rending moments as they tried to identify the dead from any clothes they may have been wearing, or any visible scar. The bodies were so horrible in appearance that the families consented to having them interred immediately; and as the funerals were held from July to the middle of September there were heart-breaking scenes.

Eventually by 19th. September ninety bodies were found, all were interred in single graves at Heworth Church Yard. One body was never found; even when eventually the Colliery commenced day to day working once more. A meeting was held at Heyworth on Wednesday 28th. May, to organize a fund for the relief of the miner's families; subscriptions came from all over Tyneside and Durham, the Coal Trade of Tyne and Wear, and also the Coal Factors of London. By 29th.December 1812, the fund; although just commenced stood at £2742, with donations arriving daily.

An alarming fact that I found when checking on the dead at Felling was that twenty six of the dead were under fourteen years of age; including two nine year olds and two eight year olds ******

TRIMDON COLLIERY 1882

On 16th. February 1882 at about 2.30 pm there was a terrible explosion at Trimdon Colliery; where sixty Eight men and boys died, along with eleven horses and ponies; six other people at East Hetton Colliery which adjoined Trimdon Colliery also died. Two of the men from East Hetton were Mr. H.C. Schier, Under Manager and Thomas Blenkinsop who was a Master Waste man. They descended from East Hetton side in an attempt to rescue some of the men, but they were killed themselves because of afterdamp gas.

The explosion in its entirety was confined to workings in the Harvey seam; which lay at a depth of 286 yards. The Low Main was bored to a depth of 194 yards and was unaffected by the blast. The downcast shaft was twelve feet in diameter and sunk a few yards below the Harvey; the cages which brought the men to the surface, ran on wire rope guides. The shaft was generally wet, and the up cast shaft lay forty yards to the east of the downcast, being sunk to the Low Main seam only. This shaft was just short of fourteen feet in diameter; there was a staple ten feet in diameter, ninety-two feet deep, sunk from the Low Main to the Harvey Seam, near to the up cast shaft and there was also an up cast shaft from the Harvey.

From the downcast shaft the haulage roads extended north and south; the districts to the south of the shaft were not affected by the blast. On the west side of the shafts there were three districts, 'The Headways', 'The Cross Cut', and the 'Narrow Board'. There was an engine near the shaft, which worked a 'Main and Tail' haulage system, from the landing. The whole of the ventilation of the pit was operated by a furnace in the Harvey seam, at the bottom of the up cast staple. This furnace was fed by return air from the plane of the explosion; a furnace man was in attendance and there was nothing near the furnace that would cause an explosion. The air circulating in the Harvey seam measured eight days prior to the explosion was found to be 52,694 cubic feet a minute. The explosion took place during a period when the pit was working to a maximum of 100%; all of the faces were working to full capacity, with the hewers and the men responsible for getting the coal to the surface all working. The Harvey produced four hundred tons of coal a day and the thickness of the seam in the Trimdon area was three feet eight inches. All of the in bye workers used '*Davy Safety Lamps'*.. Shots were fired on the day of the explosion on coal; there were also shots fired on stone. The Management always attempted to restrict the use of shots; although the Harvey at Trimdon was thought to be only moderately fiery. Near the goaf edge, gas had been observed, these areas were in the return airways and it was also observed that the coal was dry and dusty, the roadways were also dry and dusty; these also were kept under observation. On the day of the explosion temperatures were below freezing; around about the date of the explosion some gas was observed near the goaf, and they decided to have a complete examination.

    The officials of the Colliery, the day prior to the disaster had discovered no unusual source of danger. After the explosion there was limited damage to the downcast shaft, because of the wire rope guides, there was no timber to burn so the recovery of the bodies were relatively easy and the last body was brought out within three days of the explosion. It was found that the explosion had continued in-bye to the working faces in the narrow board, and Headway districts, the travel was some 2,800 yards along the main intake haulage road. The return airways were free from blast except at doors air crossings and stopping's. The roof stone at Trimdon was found to be very sound, in general and it was found that unlike other disasters there were only a small amount of falls of stone to contend with. It was also observed that there were a few full coal tubs on the haulage way the nearest one to the shaft had been damaged and had spilled on to the side of the roadway. The air doors at First South, had their frames blown out and the trapper boy who looked after them had been blown into the vicinity of the face, and into a canvas sheet, which had been used for ventilation at the in-bye side of the wood door. At the Second South, the door frames were observed twenty yards nearer to the face than the doors should be; at the Third South the door was shattered but apparently not displaced, all of the stopping's along the haulage road were displaced and the Wagon Wayman's tools were blown in-bye and spread along the roadway.

    Trimdon Grange Colliery was sunk in 1840 and was owned, together

Troubled Collieries

with Kelloe, by the (East Hetton Coal Company), but after a while was purchased by Walter Scott of Newcastle. Trimdon Grange had two shafts to the Low Main and Harvey, brought together with a staple. There was also a passageway linked to Kelloe Pit, and it was always known to be a dusty Pit. On the 16th. Of February 1882 a Barometric pressure reading was very low, with a recorded drop of 5 degrees at the pit shaft. The back shift was at present in the pit, and there were 5 deputies, 64 Hewers, 25 boys, in their work places. A caution board was posted so that out-bye, the drivers could use open midges, Davy Lamps, which had a sliding shield were also used. Although in general the roof at Trimdon had always been reported as sound; There was a high possibility that after a roof fall in the Harvey, Gas had been released into the airways. This progressed on to the work areas, mixed with coal dust, and possibly ignited from a Davy Lamp; though a later enquiry failed to substantiate this. Three men had tried to escape, from where they were working, before the actual explosion happened, at 2.40pm, but they had died close to where they worked. It appeared that the Explosion had started in 2nd. South. All of the men working in the Pit Narrow Board District, were killed, all having burns, others by the actual violence of the blast, the after-damp scattered men all over the pit, causing further deaths.

Later it was found that the explosion had damaged the Ropes and the cages; the dividing door between Kelloe and Trimdon had been blown off completely. The Harvey area was cleared of Debris, starting at the shaft end, and the rescue party progressed to the coal seams. After some hard work they eventually found the 30 Hewers in the Low Main, who were not hurt and they were brought to bank. As earlier stated, The Under-Manager of Kelloe, Herman Schier led a party from the Kelloe end, searching for survivors; as they progressed through the passageway. The After-damp seemed all around them when Thomas Blenkinsop, the Master Waste man collapsed and Skhier caught him, on trying to drag him out he also collapsed. The others eventually managed to drag them out, but both were dead. 74 men and boys died, this included the men from Kelloe, Blenkinsop and Skhier. Three brothers, George Burnett, 19, shafts man, James Burnett, 17 landing minder, who was only identified by his clothing, Joseph Burnett, hand putter, who's body was found later. The Burnett boys were mentioned in Tommy Armstrong's poem, which he wrote trying to raise funds for widows and orphans, and later a street was called Burnett Crescent, in Kelloe.

There was a long enquiry on the causes, after the funerals of the victims; most of the families and miners thought that it was a record of inhuman and greedy pit owners who just did not care. A wheel was erected to commemorate the tragedy, when half of the men folk had been killed or injured in the village, and dedicated by the Bishop of Durham.

Let us Think of Mrs. Burnett,
Once had sons, but now has none,
By the Trimdon Grange Explosion
Joseph, George, and James are gone:

A ten-year-old boy David Irvine, obviously one of the victims, summed the disaster up by writing what he thought of the explosion.

The Mine Disaster

Yesterday it happened,
So quickly, so sickly,
Trying to get out,
They were yelling
'HELP US'
But by the time they helped them
It was just too late.
My brother, cousin and my next door
Neighbour lying here beside, safe
And sound beside me in the hospital.
Some I know died in pain
With a broken body.
Some I know died helping,
Helping others to get free.

David Irvine

The whole disaster was finally noted by **Sam Cairns** with his few lines from the heart……..

REMEMBER THE FORGOTTEN
In the shadow of a mine stands a graveyard,
Where lies countless boxes of memories,
In a field full of friends.

Troubled Collieries

Over-shadowed by the spirits, of the men who,
Laughed...cried...lived & died.
Thus becoming another box of memories,
In a field full of friends. *********
Because of the nature of some of the injuries sustained by some of the dead, and with due consideration to relations, the Author had no alternative but to disregard some evidence available to him.

Trimdon Grange **High Street & Colliery**

Troubled Collieries

Trimdon Grange Memorial, to the 74 dead. Made from an actual
pit top wheel, saved after closure in 1968. This and other memorials can be seen at 'St Albans Church yard . There is also a memorial to the dead of both wars

Troubled Collieries

A very old list of the dead, also mentions the authors relation, The Master Waste Man', Thomas Blenkinsop, from Cassop: kindly given to me by Robin Walton.

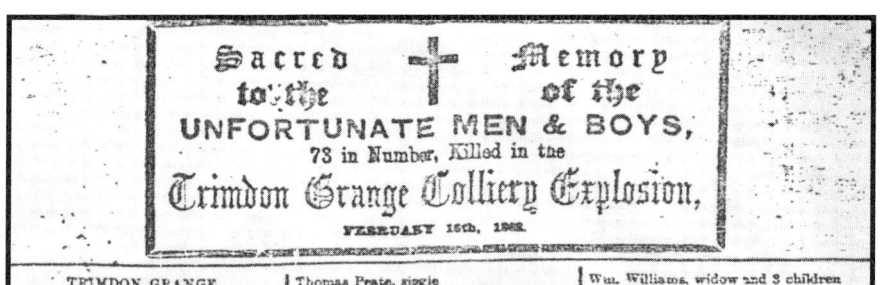

Sacred ✝ Memory to the of the UNFORTUNATE MEN & BOYS, 73 in Number, Killed in the Trimdon Grange Colliery Explosion,

FEBRUARY 16th, 1882.

TRIMDON GRANGE.
Wm. Robinson (deputy), widow & 1 child
John Errington, widow and 3 children
Samuel Richardson, single
James Stobbs, widow and 3 children
Thomas Priestley, widow and 1 child
John Douglass, boy
Thomas Sharp, single
John Hughes, single
Thomas Hunter, widow and 6 children
Andrew Smith, single
Cornelius Jones, boy
Robert Soulsby, widow
Joseph Hyde, single
John Ramsay, single
Joseph Dormand, boy
Thomas Dormand, boy
William Jefferson, boy
George Jefferson, single
John Allison, single
Henry Burke, widow and 4 children
Edward Spencer, single
George Wigham, widow and 3 children
Fred Bower, widow and 2 children
Wm. Mandally, widow
John Williams, widow and 1 child

Thomas Peate, single
George Richardson, widow and 2 children
Michael Hart, widow and 7 children
Thos. Horden (back overman), widow and up-grown family
George Lishman, single
William Bowen, boy
John Wilson, widow and 3 children
Ralph Robinson, single
Robert Edwards, single
David Edwards, single
Jacob Soulsby, widow
John Wilson (Beaton), single
Matthew Day, boy
Henry Joice, boy
Richard Thwaites (deputy), widow
George Dobson, single
Enoch Sayers, 13, single
R. Mercer, boy
Richard Dowe, single
David Griffith, single
John Edmund, boy
William Parker, boy
John Jones

TRIMDON COLLIERY.
William Hyde, widow and 1 child

Wm. Williams, widow and 3 children
Henry Miller, single
John Smith, widow and 2 children
Thomas Prior, single
Thos. Clark, widow and 2 children
Wm. Walker, widow and 2 children
Michael Docherty, single
Joseph Barnett, 22, single ⎫
George Barnett, 19, single ⎬ brothers
James Barnett, 17, single ⎭
Robert Maitland, widow and 3 children
Matthew French, boy

OLD TRIMDON.
James Boyd, boy
Michael McCail, 22, single ⎫
John McCail, 17, single ⎬ brothers
Thomas McCail, 13, single ⎭
William Jennings, boy
Patrick Dorking, boy

KELLOE (East Hetton).
Herman Schier, under-viewer
George Slack, single
Thos. Blenkinsopp, widow and 4 children
Jacob Barryman, widow and 3 children
Christopher Prest, widow and 3 children
Frank Earnshaw, single

Tune—"Poor Little Joe."

Another disaster our ears does assail,
A terrible explosion—a heart-rending tale.
Fire-damp and gas, which none can foresee,
To many a home has brought sad misery.
At Trimdon Grange Colliery, a few days ago,
An explosion occurred, filling each one with woe.
Many were cheerful that bright afternoon
When the dread sound was heard, filling each home
 [with gloom.

Chorus—
At Trimdon Grange Colliery,—most sad is the tale,
Poor widows and orphans in sorrow bewail.
For those dear ones who're dead now many will mourn,
Seventy poor souls to Eternity gone.

When the fatal explosion it did rend the air,
Poor mothers and children rush'd forth in dispair
To seek for those loved ones who were down below.
Most heart-rending tidings they soon were to know.
"O, where is my husband?" "O, where are my sons?"
"They're dead," came the answer to those anxious ones.
The disaster so sudden no warning it gave,
But sent those brave souls to an untimely grave.

Brave men volunteer'd from the collieries around
To bring up the dead from the dark underground,
When they were o'ertaken by the treacherous fire-damp,
In the cold arms of death two were brought up to bank.

Around the pit mouth many tears then were shed
For the loss of those brave ones now cold and dead.
God help the widows and orphans we pray,
Now the husbands and fathers they have passed away.

Some homes have lost one, and others lost two,
While two mothers miss three sons from their view.
What will they do, now the bread-winners gone.
May Heaven send comfort for those left to mourn.
May those who have plenty bestow a small share
For the fatherless children bowed down in despair.
Their homes once so cheerful with woe does abound
For the memory of those who were killed underground.

There's scarcely a day passes over our head
Without some disaster to fill us with dread.
Brave men cut off in the deep fiery mine
While toiling for bread with no gleam of sunshine.
When the cage is descending they never do know
If alive they'll return or perish below.
When the gas overtakes them they're doomed to die,
All retreat is cut off—escape is not nigh.

May God in His mercy look down from above
And comfort the widows with unbounded love.
For the lost ones there's sorrow, and suffering is great
Lamenting a husband's or son's dreadful fate.
They are gone from this world, their labour is o'er,
Let us hope with bright angels they'll dwell evermore.
The bright world above we hope they do share,
And all rest in Heaven.—there is no parting there!

Troubled Collieries

Above ***St. Pauls Trimdon Station*** and below ***St. Albans Trimdon Grange***; services for the dead miners would have been carried out at both parishes. St. Paul's is an amazing little Church with a clock tower and very small in comparison to its cemetery. *Photograph's 'The Author'*

EASINGTON COLLIERY 1951

The date was 29th. Of May 1951. It was on this day that Fire Damp, was ignited by a Cutter Machine pick. The Firedamp was released from the goaf, and it was reported that the explosion was strengthened by the ignition of coal dust, from a conveyor belt in the Duckbill District about 1¼ mile from the shaft bottom. An observant Waggon-Wayman heard a loud bang and quickly got the men in the area out to safety, and where there was plenty of air to counteract the gas. The Waggon-Wayman also had the sense to warn the mine officials and namely the under manager, he also tried to get in touch with the Duckbill district but was not able to do this. The manager informed the rescue services who quickly rushed to the area.

The rescuers quickly organized themselves and started to precede in-bye, but to their horror found that there had been a roof-fall over a very wide area. By this time a very large crowd started to congregate at the top of the pithead and in a number of ways hindered the rescue attempts. A lamp was found in the area of the shaft belonging to Ronnie Ritchie, and rescuers at first thought that that he must be missing, but apparently the Waggon-Wayman had borrowed the lamp, so that he could warn other districts, and he had sent Ritchie to the shaft where there was light and fresh air. Later he said that he thought something terrible had happened because all of the lights had gone out, and there was a high amount of dust in the air. There was also a strange sense of apprehension. People at the pithead would not go home and even after 10 PM, were still congregating waiting for news of loved one's. Mr. Watson, (miner's leader) finally had to speak to them, telling them to return to their homes and pray. Some did go home but others who had fathers and sons in the pit would not leave the area, especially when there was a little hope. The explosion was heard in the seam below the five-quarter seam; they had never heard anything like it, it was like a muffled bang that shook the whole area; there was a general feeling that they were glad it did not seem to be happening where they were situated. The officials started to withdraw the men very orderly and it reminded miners of Dunkirk all over again. As the men slowly made their way towards the shaft a black cloud of dust came towards them from the stricken Five-Quarter to their seam which was 'The Main Coal'. At the landing of the main coal deputies took no chance and hurried the withdrawal out of the pit as quickly possible; the mines rescue team again had been urgently sent for.

The 'Duckbill', district was in the north pit's 'Five Quarter', seam and this is where the disaster started. Men said that the Ducks was hard to get into and hard to get coal out of. The seam was serviced by a string of conveyor belts; one continually delivering and emptying onto another going into a different direction. The dust lay heavy in the air as the coal tipped on to another belt continuing the process out bye. All of the time coal spilled onto the wagon way; timber leaders had a difficult job taking timber roof supports into the forward coal faces. Huge deposits of coal were evident. The more stone dust that was put on, the more coal dust was spilt and it was just a waste of time. Miners going in-bye could see the particles of dust in the ray shone by their lamps; all knew that this is what they were breathing. One miner described being in the ducks area just days before the explosion. He checked with his safety lamp and found that his flame area filled up with flame, which indicated a high percentage of gas. This shocked him so much he accidentally dropped his lamp. It was a frightening experience for the man, but all he could do was to report it; other men told of 'Spiral alarms', could not be carried as they continually went off. This was a recipe for disaster but for all of this men continued working day after day, never dreaming that one day the seam would explode.

As the emergency call was received by the one man on duty at the rescue station at Houghton-Le-Spring, he made further calls to Crook and Ashington. Five men quickly boarded the Thorneycroft, which had been converted to transport the rescuers and their equipment, which consisted of twelve sets of breathing equipment. The men were totally independent having their own lamps and safety equipment; all they needed was permission from the manager to proceed underground. The men who went to Easington that day were permanently at Houghton for this reason alone;

they were Dobson, Stanfield, Jimmy Armstrong, A.S. Adamson, & George Rafter. At just about six in the morning there was not a lot of traffic on the roads and it did not take long to get to Easington. Most of the men were apprehensive as most had no experience of any explosion but hoped their training would be enough to guide them through. Easington was a very large colliery and employed many men. Within sixteen minutes they arrived at the colliery gates where the manager was waiting with six other officials. No one else was about, as news had not yet got out. On arrival even the manager was vague on just what had happened; he went on to say that there had been a blow out shot and he estimated wrongly that there was some twenty men in the area. The rescue team filled up with liquid air and they proceeded underground. Everything was black as night as there was no lighting at all and the lamps were put straight on in the cage reflecting uncertain looks on the men's faces.

On arrival at the shaft bottom they quickly preceded in-bye carrying their oil lamps, but because of a high degree of gas they no longer were able to carry them because of filling up with dangerous flame. The dust had settled on the roadways and it had caked on roof supports. It was a strange sensation as there was no air and everything was deathly silent. The air in the pit was hanging thick and stagnant. Well in towards the faces they came across a tremendous fall of stone and the force of the explosion could be imagined. There was just no way through. The men re-traced their steps meeting the manager on the way, who informed them of the terrible facts that at the time they were not aware of. The disaster was worse than first thought and in fact there were between sixty and eighty men beyond the fall. The manager also informed the rescue team of an alternative way in. By now the rescuers wanted some success and they set out with determination to get into the stricken area, marking their progress with chalk as they went so that the next rescue team knew which way they had gone.

After their time was up the Houghton men returned to the surface for a break and the Crook team took over. Finally with determination and a few mishaps they managed to get to the deputies Kist where they found absolute carnage. The men had been just about to change shifts and they had gathered at the Kist for instructions. Twenty men were laid dead; the rescuers checked each one for any sign of life. Shot firers detonators were strewn about the area and these were carefully collected. They started to get the dead out of the pit, later they were put in canvas bags and then in canisters. Later rescuers worked without their breathing equipment and used dettol swabs to cover their mouths and noses to counter the smell of the bodies. The men toiled relentlessly working twelve hours on and twelve off. It was heart breaking; the dead were all just young lads mostly fillers one rescue worker knew some of them and he murmured that hardly any were over thirty. All good North men whose families had been miners in the area for years; men with young wives and children. The rescuers picked their way further in-bye to the face they managed to get a further 175 yards in-between falls of stone when they found a further 26 bodies which left a further 18 missing; the men progressed further coming across still more falls of stone and this is where Henry Burdess [41] from Brancepeth Colliery collapsed even though he was using breathing equipment. His colleagues tried to revive him to no avail; artificial respiration had no effect on him. Henry was a very respected miner from Brancepeth and liked by everyone.

  Earlier another rescuer had died while attempting to get miners out; his name was T.Y. Wallace of Deneside, Seaham. He had only been married for two months and now he had given up his life for his fellow men. The crowd at the pit top began to increase as the men who usually worked at this time started to congregate, and waited for news, the crowd had swelled to 2800, some having fathers husbands and brothers others friends and neighbours. A Lily white racing pigeon was noted flying above the pithead and some of the men said it belonged to Jack Wilson who was a five-Quarter engine man and who was missing. The 'Salvation Army' van, handed out cups of tea to the people waiting for news; there were also smiles and words of comfort. It was noticeable that a young girl also waited patiently; she was waiting for news of Stephen Hunt, whom she was due to marry in a fortnight's time. Stephen and two of his uncles were also missing. Mrs. McRoy waited for a second time in her life, her husband had been posted missing presumed dead once before when he spent the rest of the war as a prisoner; now he was missing again. All they could do now was wait for news.

  Underground the rescuers having lost two men were taking no more chances. They could not proceed any further until a 'fresh air base', had been established and this base was essential because of afterdamp gas. It was generally thought that they would not find any more men alive. Sam Watson addressed the crowd at the pithead asking them to return to their homes, as there would be no further bulletins. Mr. Arthur Horner (General secretary of (NUM) arrived also Lord Hyndley (Chairman NCB) also Mr. Shinwell at the time defence secretary and MP for Easington was arriving that day. By now there was twelve rescue teams working in two hour on and two off, 1000 feet below the ground where the airways were still full of poisoned gas. The rescuers worked one and a half miles in-bye bringing out the dead. Volunteers from the ordinary miners at the pit were a godsend for the teams bringing tea and sandwiches. These men also worked hard to clear the fall of stone so that the bodies could be recovered.

Forty hours after the explosion twenty-one of the eighty victims had been accounted for; sixty were still missing. The first north was checked right up to the coalface and none were found. It was thought that the rest would be found further in. The blast had ruptured the ventilation system and this slowed recovery work and hopes of finding anyone alive were very remote. At the surface Sam Watson read out the names of the missing, Alan Joyce stood with mixed emotions, he heard his mates names called out, Billy Kelly, Bert. Burns, Peter Lynch, that fateful morning Alan had over slept, missing the last cage later a friend called to tell his wife that he was missing and found him eating his breakfast.

The rescue workers had managed to get passed the fall, where they found Mattie. Williams he was just alive; he was laid behind some tubs. They put him on a stretcher and carried him straight out-bye but later he died in hospital. The point of the explosion had came right to the main way because men in this area had died of horrific burns which included Mattie. Williams who it appeared had been busy putting tokens on the set. As time went on hope that any more of the sixty miners would be found alive was remote; the rescue services thought that even if one person could be found alive then it would make the rescuers feel a little better but it was not to be. When viewing the roadway later it was generally thought because of the force and violence of the explosion no one could survive. The area was a complete shambles, tubs and roof supports were blown to bits this included the miner's bodies it was a very sad day at Easington indeed.

An official list of dependants of the twenty-four men found, and fifty-seven still unaccounted for, was made when a check was completed on miner's homes. Since the explosion fifteen different rescue teams had been used working six-hour tours of duty. Seventy fresh and different men came from other collieries. Work began on the final 450 yards towards the coalface; one more body was found but not identified. There were 2800 men laid idle from the colliery because of the disaster and it was agreed that they get a guaranteed minimum wage. Wages due to the victims were to be paid to the dependants. An investigation into the causes and other circumstances would later be arranged.

Aftermath

The work of bringing the bodies to the surface carried on until Friday 8th. June. Nine bodies were still missing; rescue work had carried on for 256 hours, sixty brigade staff being used along with 291 rescue workers losing two men. Subject to consent of the bereaved families all eighty-one miners who died at Easington will share a common grave, 'Easington Miners Lodge' announced this. The clergy and the other sympathisers were in agreement as long as various denominations were considered. A colliery band will play at the graveside when the closing hymn would be '*Gresford*', written by Robert Saint of Jarrow. Services were arranged as follows Saturday June 2nd. Twelve noon Salvation Army, 1pm. Methodists, 2pm. Roman Catholics, 3pm. Church of England. Notices will be posted at the welfare hall and the other churches mentioned; places at each service will be reserved for immediate relatives and the public are requested to allow these to be seated first. Easington Colliery re-opened starting night shift Monday 11th. June the last body was accounted for on Thursday 14th June. Every precaution was taken in testing for gas and the pit in all areas was found to be completely clear. The odd one or two bodies were all eventually found, men seemed to be drawn to where these poor men were buried.

At the time of the explosion The Duckbill area was found by the rescuers to be full of after-damp gas, and the whole area had to be ventilated before the rescuers could enter, two of the rescuers who suffered with emphysema, struggled to breath and in fact inhaled some gas, both men collapsed and died. The disaster at Easington was a terrible waste of life and seventy two miners were found dead, four of which could not be identified, nine others were also found, and then two rescue workers were buried elsewhere.

Fifty Years on:

The date was Monday May 28th. 2001 exactly fifty years since that terrible day on May 29th. 1951, when an explosion ripped through the Five Quarter seam at Easington Colliery. At the time the weather was beautiful and people were starting to think of their annual holidays which most in the area would spend locally at Easington which was situated right on a beautiful part of the North East coast. It was 3.30 in the morning and two shifts merged bringing eighty one men together as the daily shifts were changing at the 'Duck Bill' area none of these men would see their homes again all would have a terrible violent death. A later enquiry found that at 4.20 that morning a cutter struck *'Pyrites'*, which ignited 'Firedamp', gas, causing a massive explosion, which brought down 120 yards of roof as if it was butter. Louis Brennan manned the Cutter machine on this fateful morning; Louis left a wife and six children; there were three boys and three girls; the oldest, Peter was serving with the 'Engineers', part of the 'British Forces', in Malaya and stationed at the time in Singapore. Peter was flown home on compassionate grounds. Michael Brennan was nine years of age at the time of this terrible accident; Michael and his father were close, involved in everything going in the area and his death affected him tremendously the family now live at Aycliffe Village, Co. Durham. Michael's mother on no account would allow Michael to work at the pit; after going to secondary school he went on to serve in the 'Coldstream Guards', then later in the police force, where he finished his working life. The men were entombed in a hell of deadly fumes. The late reverend Beddows who was vicar in 1951 said the men and their memory will be commemorated in the hearts of the Easington people; they were representatives of the finest men in the Durham Coalfield.

 Shortly a memorial garden will be opened which has been created on the colliery site overlooking the sea; £100,000 has been spent on the new garden and improving the cemetery. New features have been added which included two sets of crossed picks and five bronze miners lamps; Easington's MP John Cummings will unveil these. The Bishop of Durham Rev. Michael Turnbull will conduct a graveside blessing; the Chairman of Easington Parish Council Coun. Alan Burnip will unveil a plaque and Easington Colliery band will perform a specially commissioned piece of music.

 The garden has been created to represent the colliery; a pit wheel has been installed at the centre of a flowerbed and the footpath represents the three-tier pit cage. There are small ingots on the footpath that represents the miner's tokens each, with individual designs by local school children; lines of poetry are to be seen around the garden explaining what it is like to work in a mine. The entrance gates, which were produced by Michael Johnson, are based on the banner of Easingtons miners lodge and a time line runs from the park to where the shaft was, representing the depth of the pit shaft,

Troubled Collieries

which was 342 metres. Funding for the project came from the coal industry Social Welfare Organization, Durham NUM., Coalfields Generation Trust, and Easington Colliery Parish Council, Turning the Tide & Unison. The event will start with a blessing and unveiling, then a service at the Church of Ascension. There will be a graveside service. The organizers hoped that everyone having any connection at all with the disaster would attend.

Easington Village Crossroads; below St. Mary the Virgin Church:

Troubled Collieries

Top Picture** carrying out the dead; below the devastation from the force of the **blast: Pictures Newcastle Chronicle

Troubled Collieries

<u>The dead at Easington</u>

Troubled Collieries

THE ROLL CALL OF THE DEAD

John Anson, William Armstrong, Mark Bedding, Matthew Blevins, George Brenkley, Thomas Brenkley, Louis Brennan, George Miller Brown, Henry Burdess, Bertram Burn, Emmerson Cain, Frederick Cairns, George Calvert, James Calvin, Frederick Carr, George William Carr, James Carr, John Edward Challoner, Richard Champley, Albert Kerr Chapman, Joseph Charlton, John Clough, William Arthur Dryden, John Ellison, Charles Fishburn, Henry Fishburn, Thomas Garside, Joseph Godsman, Albert Gowland, George Goulburn, Ernest Goyns, Herbert Goyns, John Harker, John William Henderson, Thomas Hepple, Daniel Hunt, Stephen Hunt, William Hunt, Arthur Chambers Hutton, Frederick Ernest Jepson, Herbert Jeffrey Jobling, Lawrence Jones, Thomas Edward Jones, John Kelly, William Kelly, John Edward Armstrong Lamb, Jesse Stephenson Link, Joseph Fairless Lippeatt, Peter Lynch, Dennis McRoy, William James McRoy, Robert William Milburn, Harold Nelson, Albert Newcombe, Norman Nicholson, Robert Noble, William Edward Forbes Parks, William Parkin, Robert Pase, Stanley Peaceful, Alexander Penman, John Thomas Porter, James Porter, Thomas Valentine Rice, John Robinson, John George Robinson, George Scott, Albert Seymour, Frederick Sillito, George Henry Stubbs, Matthew White Surtees, Hugh Bell Surtees, Laurence Thompson, Thomas Thompson, Thomas Trisnan, Robert Turnbull, Jack Young Wallace, George Wilkie, Reginald Wilkinson, Matthew Williams, Robert Willis, John Wilson, Stephen Wilson

BRANCEPETH COLLIERY
<u>1896</u>

Joseph & John Straker from South Shields part owned Willington Colliery with Joseph Love who lived in a large mansion type house at Willington very near to the Colliery. The same people sank a further Colliery 'Brancepeth', around 1850. The amazing thing about the two Collieries were that Willington was nearer to Brancepeth Colliery than Willington Colliery, which was situated near to Brancepeth. As Brancepeth started to produce coal the population rose from 258 to 965 with a total of 159 houses.

The Colliery was sunk to 240 feet and eventually consolidated with the Collieries of Sunnybrow, Meadowfield, Brandon, Oakenshaw and Bolden the last mentioned closing in 1931. The Company controlling the Collieries traded as 'Straker & Love'. Brancepeth Colliery was situated parallel to the Willington & Durham Railway to a mile towards Brancepeth Village.

Coal was dispatched until 1930 from hoppers situated close to Willington where the coal was distributed to all types of haulage including the Railways. Enormous waste heaps were very apparent on the opposite of the railway line and it wasn't until the 60s that they were leveled and landscaped. It was also worth noting that Brancepeth was known to have the largest Coking Works in the World, having 990 Coke ovens. The Colliery was very profitable but it was not without problems.

Explosion
An explosion occurred at the Colliery about 11 PM on Monday evening the 13th. April when 17 miners lost their lives. At this time a three-shift system was in operation, the sequence beginning at 5am. until 10; then 10 until 4; the final shift consisted of stone men, shifters and deputies their job was to repair and prepare the Colliery for the following day. One

consolation regarding the timing of the explosion was that if the Colliery had fired on the day shift then approximately 150 men and boys would most certainly have been involved. Previous to this day there had been no indication that an explosion was apparent; Brancepeth had always been known as a safe pit. The Engine Man working on the late shift first indicated that there were problems below ground. There was a tremendous blast and an out rush of air at the mouth of the mine which was described just like a tornado. The officials quickly informed the Manager, Mr. Grieves that something was wrong below ground.

    A rescue party was quickly organised and they descended the shaft. There was one consolation in that the shaft was more or less sound. A set of tubs stationary in the landing adjacent to the shaft took the full force of the blast leaving the shaft intact. Other stopping including a large brick arch was not so lucky and was blown into fragments. First indications were that the blast had started in the Brockwell seam, which extended for three miles distance from the shaft. Because the brick stopping had been blown out, the air in the pit was foul. There were further indications that pointed to the explosion starting in the 'Daisy Drift'.

    The blast and ground tremor had been heard and felt as far away as Crook, and even Tudhoe and areas around. Tudhoe were apparently in a direct line with Brancepeth Brockwell, and an air rush was felt. The Managers of Brancepeth Mr. Grieves and Mr. Weeks were first to respond to the explosion and headed a party of very experienced officials, John Rutherford, (Engineer), Mr. Lawson (Fore Over man) Mr. Laws (back over man), this party headed a further fifteen others all very experience miners. As the news spread scores of other experienced engineers, sinkers and miners, rushed to the pithead.

    Below ground it was sheer carnage; there were roof falls over a large area. Four boys employed near to the shaft bottom on pumping operations had travelled to another job about two miles further in-bye these were **Thomas Blackett**, **James Mullen** and **Thomas Cunningham** they were all aged between fourteen and seventeen. Also with them was **William Bird**, 13, son of John Bird. At their new job they felt a strong wind, which put out their lamps and candles. The boys roamed about in the dark and were not able to find their way back to the shaft. They were in complete darkness and climbed over falls of roof. Finally they saw lights coming towards them which were the rescue party. Two over-men took them to bank; although they felt sick with the after-damp they quickly got over their

Troubled Collieries

adventure **George Wilson** a married man with a grown up family was blown over and on to some steel plates and was injured; he too was taken to bank. The rescue party finally reached the Brockwell; the whole of the area and obviously the seat of the explosion was wrecked. There were falls of stone everywhere, coal tubs were smashed, even steel Couplings had snapped like butter with the force of the explosion. Men worked frantically to find survivors with picks and shovels knowing time was the essence; finally fumes exhausted them and sheer fatigue; others had to take their places. One over-man John Gilchrist who had travelled from Brandon crawled over a fall of stone and fell badly over the other side after being over come by after-damp. His companions bravely formed a chain by holding hands and dragged the man away from danger in an unconscious state. He was sent for medical attention when he soon recovered. Conditions in the pit became increasingly difficult to make even the slightest progress. Some spaces were hard to negotiate and young fit small-framed youth's were brought forward to help out and negotiate areas where larger framed men found it impossible.

Mr. Weeks and others tried to reach the miners from the Oakenshaw Pit but found this impossible from there and returned to Brancepeth. A large amount of timber and bricks were sent down the Colliery to replace timber and roof stopping that had been blown out because of the blast. Mr. Grieves and Weeks were ordered by Doctors to go home and rest as they had been in the pit from early Monday morning and had worked none stop to find survivors. Other High Ranking officials from other Collieries filled their places they were John Wilson, (MP Durham), Mr. E. Douglas (Manager Crook), Mr. H.F. Cox (Manager Thornley) they had descended the shaft and offered valuable assistance.

Other Rescuers who had worked none stop were now exhausted and were forced to go to the surface they had to return through countless roof falls and foul air. Other enthusiastic miners filled their places; disregarding many dangers. Tuesday morning at 5.30 am. the rescuers had found **Joseph Foster** he was aged 40, he had been badly mauled by the explosion; **John Rogerson** aged 66 was found he was a 'Master Shifter', and in charge of all in that shift. **Thomas Nicholson** aged 20 of Catharine Street, was in his second shift at the Colliery and was newly married; his wife was extremely distressed. A further three bodies were found, **Bartholomew Newell** aged 15; **Michael Turner**, 50; he had a handkerchief tied round his mouth and Joseph Foster had a piece of cloth in his mouth. One of the men had his mouth to a piece of metal plate trying to suck the moisture. This was an old fashioned antidote for gas poisoning. It seemed all had struggled hard to stay alive all in vane and they had lost their battle. All were put into canvas bags, put onto stretchers and waited their turn to go to the surface. Joiners were working all hours to complete making coffins for the poor men.

On Wednesday morning more bodies were found, **John R. Dawson** aged 20, single. His father was one of the first volunteers to look for survivors, when he discovered his own son. It was said that young John was an excellent footballer playing in the Bishop Auckland district. **Ralph Lawson** was aged 60, **Jim Jefferson** 58, and **Robert Hanson** aged 15. The latter two had run for their lives and were found in the 'Dairy Flat', their bodies clean and un-marked. **Thomas Carling** aged 14, was said to have missed the blast but died from after damp poisoning. His father had also sadly died three years ago.

William Cook 52, and **Henry Hodgeson** were found; they actually were found Tuesday but were situated in a dangerous area just beyond reach. Stone hung dangerously overhead; their bodies were recovered Thursday. **J. Henry Hodgeson** was found the immediate area where he was found had to be made safe before his recovery. Henry had just qualified in an examination for mine management, getting a first class certificate. His brother who also identified his nephew, **Thomas Carling**, identified him. **Robert Hanson**, and **John Wearmouth** aged 64 were found Saturday morning

By noon Sunday morning April the 19th. there were still bodies to be found; afterdamp was still very apparent and men were affected tremendously. The rescuers reached the top of the hitch at the Daisy Workings; in this area the afterdamp was very bad and most rescuers had to be replaced by young and fresh men. A very large roof fall had blocked the return airway at the 'Daisy Working's', and it slowed progress down; the new squad managed to clear this after which they found another 5 bodies. **Thomas Lawson** was found behind some tubs. The men found here seemed to be trying to vacate the area; all had their jackets on and were proceeding towards the shaft. When caught by the after-damp gas. The men were not affected by blast but were a little swollen by the gas. All were placed in canvas bags to wait their turn to be taken to the surface.

Charles Lintern was identified aged 34, this was his second shift as a stone man, 3 days previously Charles had worked with his brother Frank who was a strong and fast worker and Charles could not keep up the pace.

His brother wanted him to stay with him saying that he did not mind, and was prepared to share the money made, equally. Charles insisted that he go with the stone men on the easier job and this resulted in his death. **Charles Lintern's** wife was expecting a baby and it would be her sixth child. News of her husband's death had a terrible affect on her. **George W. Lawther** aged 39, was married with five children; **Trisran Spence** aged 31, this was the second fatality in the family three years previously his father had been killed by a fall of stone.

It was noted that the father of **William Laws** in company with his two other sons were waiting at Bank. He was an overman and had been in the pit all day searching for William. **William Rawlings** aged 50 of Albert Street, was found. He was married with one child; one other son had been killed with a broken back just a short time ago. Twenty bodies were now found; it was said that **William Laws** died later while at home. The Doctor sent William Flemming to Bank; after he had been overcome with afterdamp, while searching the 'Jet', after trying to rescue **Ralph Lawson**. William was wrapped in blankets and carried to the surface on a stretcher where he was put to bed.

After news of the explosion spread round the village people began to gather at the 'Pit Head', fearing for their loved one's. Mr. D. Atkinson a Police Sergeant stationed at Willington sent a messenger to Durham, informing them of the explosion. Soon a force of Police arrived in the area to make sure everything was done in an orderly fashion. Woman stood all night waiting for news, youngsters clinging to their skirts. People arrived from all over the County and even further a field; they came in ponies and traps, train, bicycles and even walked to the area. At that time the population was in the region of 7000. Superintendent Burrell who controlled the force of Police said that the crowd was excellent. Everyone silently watched the action of the Shaft pulley wheels searching faces for any news at all. Doctor Brown was seen to be circulating making sure that any one requiring medical attention received it.

Word came that the first body would be coming to the surface; this was Joseph Foster; he was taken to a makeshift Morgue which was a storeroom. This is where the bodies could be identified; on one occasion two women claimed the same body. Mr. J. H. Straker on behalf of the owners expressed great sorrow that so dreadful a calamity should have fallen on them; he went on to say that there was nothing in the history of the Colliery that there was any cause to fear anything, and they could only express their great regret that the explosion happened. Everything possible was being done to alleviate the sorrow of the relatives would be done

Funerals Over the next few weeks' funerals were held for the deceased men. Words could not describe the terrible scenes of people mourning their dead. The Churches of Primitive Methodism, Presbyterian, and Wesleyan were very busy. Tom Carling aged 14 was carried to the Church by four young friends to the Catholic Church of 'Our Lady of Perpetual Succor', he was the only Catholic to lose his life in the Explosion. There was a co-incidence in the death in that Tom's sister was due to marry John Martin in this very Church; but due to inflammation and Pleurisy John had died just prior to the explosion. Both boys were buried in the same grave; John Martin lowered first. The priest father Holsten was moved to tears when mentioning 'Our little Carling', who was an excellent member of the Church. He served on the Alter like an angel and was never late for mass. High Mass was sung.

400 people attended Thomas Nicholson's funeral; Rev. M.M. Robson Presbyterian, Rev. R. Huddleston, (Primitive Methodist), and Rev. W. Wonfor (Wesleyan Chapel) gave equally brilliant services. There were also 23 ponies in the pit and all died in the stables. Mr. G. Farrow (Vetnary Surgeon) tried to reach them but was stopped by bad roof falls. Eventually men cleared a way through and the ponies were brought to the surface and buried in a field. One young driver waited for the ponies patiently picking out his own, then crying sadly uncontrollably. He was very much attached to the animal he said, "It was the best and strongest pony in the pit"; "it never had to be asked twice to do anything". "Bobby' was always willing and faithful"

Relief Fund
Lord Boyne who owned most of the land gave £500; the Durham Miners Association gave £800, Straker & Love, £500. The 'Prudential Insurance Group', paid out on fifteen claims. The Sunnybrow Cricket Club arranged a concert at three Council Schools. The Mayor of Middlesbrough; Councilor Theo. Phillips gave generously when opening the fund. Mr. Anthony Wilkinson £25, Sir William Eden (Father of Anthony Eden), £5 many smaller donations from ordinary people were forth coming.

People
The below mentioned officials all gave their assistance to the relief fund

and helped where needed:
E. Watson, & E. Douglas, (Manager Crook). F.O Kirkup & C. Widdes, (Managers Bitchburn), E. Chivers (Official Eldon), W. Steel (Sunnybrow), M.J. Davies, (Coundon), T. Pearson (Auckland Park), H.F. Cox (Thornley), C Douglas, (White Lee), Mr. Hopkinson, (Newton Cap), C. Hendy, (Etherley), T.Y. Greener, (Pease's West), Mr. Fishwick, (Binchester).

To finish this sad part of Willington's History there must be a mention to the woman of the village most grieved for loved ones and had to carry on the sad times of bringing up their families on their own. All conducted themselves in a way that explains the roll taken by North Country Woman in the volatile and dangerous years when people depended on the coal Industry to make a living; sometimes only earning a pittance:

Inquest

The jury gave the following verdict in writing. A shot was fired by persons not known and this ignited coal dust and caused an explosion on 'Cross Cut Way'; culminating in 20 men and boys accidentally loosing their lives. They were further asked if there was any recommendation & they said that they would leave this up to the Government Inspectors:

Sacred to the Memory of

THE UNFORTUNATE MEN,

Who Lost their Lives in the Terrible

COLLIERY DISASTER, AT BRANCEPETH PIT,

APRIL 13th, 1896.

John Dowson	Henry Hodgson	Charles Linton	Tristram Spence
Thos. Nicholson	William Cooke	John Wearmouth	Thomas Carling
John Forster	George Lawther	John Jefferson	Michael Turner
John Rogerson	William Laws	Robert Ransome	Joseph Brigham
Ralph Lawson	Thomas Lawson	Wm Rawlings	Bert Newell

Troubled Collieries

New Pit, Brancepeth Colliery, seams were near to the surface & sometimes men were able to enter the pit by a drift; although the C. Pit was only accessible from the shaft. Sunk around 1870; by 1914 the pit employed 1000 people. Later blue clay was extracted for making bricks. Below Air & Water condensers at Brancepeth; management expanded into other products including coke and its by-products including tar products, sulphate of ammonia & Benzole along with gas for the use to the public at Willington and elsewhere:

Troubled Collieries

Willington Old Hall, actually 'Willington House', dates back to 1600; Joseph Love; Joint owner of Brancepeth Colliery lived here in 1850. Below Brancepeth Castle', the area is full of History; the Castle was a Neville stronghold & was forfeited to the Crown during the reign of Elizabeth 1st. In 1635, after the Northern Knights went from the Castle to place the Catholic 'Mary Queen of Scots', on the English throne. After securing Hartlepool together with ships for an escape route and clearing resistance at Barnard Castle & Richmond the army were defeated in battle near Durham by the Crown:

WINGATE GRANGE 1906

A sample bore was sunk at Roderidge by Seymour & Co. in 1840, this turned out to be a very expensive venture. It was put down on land at Catlow that had been sold by John Dobson and now owned by George Townsend Fox. The original borehole did not yield much coal at all and they sent for William Coulson. Coulson was a Master Sinker whose fame in finding coal was amazing. Coulson put down a borehole on the Catley Hall estate; finding the Busty and other rich seams without trouble. He also found that the Harvey was washed out. Coulson found a good alternative in that he found Fire Clay also containing a small amount of iron ore, which was the start of the 'Roderidge Fire Bricks', and this Company prospered right in to the present Century

The shafts passed through 87' of soil & clay 267' of Magnesium Limestone before reaching rich veins of coal. This later produced 690 tons a day employing 1,200 men and boys. Any other Sinker but Coulson would have been put off, having found so much soil, limestone and clay. The coal was of good quality and therefore in great demand. The shafts were used for ascending and descending; water was controlled from the Hutton Seam by a pumping engine pumping 650 gallons a day.

On a Sunday Evening October 14th. 1906 at precisely 11.40 there was an explosion. It started in the 'Low Main', seam. 24 men died from the blast and two others died from afterdamp gas. As the hour approached midnight word travelled through the community that the pit had fired. People rushed to the Pit Head, all watched in silence as volunteers arrived and prepared themselves to go into the pit. At first the full implications were not apparent; but indications were that many men were trapped in the Hutton and Harvey seams. This was because of the damage to the shaft and cages. There was a strange co-incidence in that other seams were not aware of any problem; they even used shots. Two stone men Tommy Luke and Geordie Robson asked 'Young', Dick Ashcroft to fire them shots in stone where they were developing; this was approx. 1am. It was possible to get food and drink to the men trapped, by lowering down a basket in a kibble. The kibble would eventually be used to vacate the men. The rescue teams worked like men possessed, calling on inner strengths, this was the North Country miner; they would not rest until they had their comrades safe and out of the pit. It was a fact that by early Tuesday morning these brilliant rescuers had all of the survivors to the surface. After nearly thirty-six hours of working none stop, the ninety-three men who had been entombed were finally brought to the surface all were alive. During Monday night seventy-nine men were brought up and yesterday (Sunday) fourteen others were rescued in small batches.

Although there were still fifteen bodies in the pit, the Inquest went ahead Tuesday. Survivors and rescuers told many heroic stories of happenings over the last hours. One old miner led men to some old workings that were free of afterdamp gas. Eventually when the survivors were found they had been standing up in water up to their waist's for eight hours. Food had run out and they had to eat corn from the mangers of the ponies. The 'Master Shifter', from the Harvey Seam who was one of the entombed men, said he had been in the pit from ten o'. Clock Sunday evening. There were around ninety men in the scam and everything seemed to be progressing well.

Around 11.50 when the air seemed to change. The Master Shifter got everyone together at the Shaft bottom and work was suspended. They found that the shaft had been damaged and men could not be taken to the surface. The earliest men could be given food was 5 pm. Monday evening and this was sent down in large quantities and very much welcomed by the starving men. Some managed to get some sleep using straw from the stables and all seemed in good health apart from the uneasy feeling of uncertainty. One man called Brown who was the rapper signaler for the seam got a blow on the head and he was not very well. Later one person who was in the Harvey said they sang hymns, particularly the boys.

Wingate Colliery 1908

A shafts man carried one

of the bravest acts out. On Monday morning he went down the shaft on top of the cage in the 'Lady Pit'. He found he could go no further when the cage stuck some way from the imprisoned men. He took the food the rest of the way by rope lowering him down to the level of the seam and thus getting food to the starving men. In the Low Main where the explosion started H. Mc Gonnell had been working over a mile in-bye; there was a sensation in the air as if someone had left the doors open and a whirlwind had been produced. They carried on working until George Harris informed them that something serious had happened, he advised them to make their way carefully out-bye to the shaft.

There were four in the party, Cuncliffe, Peat, Dawson and Mc Gonnell all went towards the shaft together. They came near to the 1st. East Way; there was an accumulation of dust and there was an eerie ghostlike sensation around the place. Five men were found all seemed to be in a deep sleep, none had any marks on them. Gunnell lifted one of them infact it was Farnworth and poured water over his face to try and revive him; others were trying to revive the rest of the men. All to no avail, Peat thought it was important that we quickly got to an area where there was good air and led us to East Way; where it was possible to breath. We all felt cold and damp and by now our lamps were going out, with the exception of Cuncliffe who's lamp lasted 18. ½. hours. After the rescuers had saved all of the survivors they began to concentrate on the dead. Most had to be carried over dangerous ground and timber which was strewn all over the place. Many had to be dug out from falls of roof. Fifteen bodies were placed in Tarpaulin and carried to the 'Five Quarter Seam'; from there brought to the surface in the cage. The dead were carried passed bareheaded solemn faced comrades to the Joiners Shop, which was used as a Mortuary. A total of twenty-four men that had died in the explosion were now accounted for. Shortly the experts started to arrive at the Colliery Mr. Claude Palmer, son of Sir Charles Palmer began to look quickly for causes of the terrible disaster. Most seemed to accept that the cause was the careless use of a naked flame.

Doctor Nixon Suffragan, Bishop of Durham visited the bereaved at Wingate; the Vicar accompanied him. When the first body appeared from the Shaft he stood bare headed and later addressed a large group of people; expressing his sympathy to the families. The explosion was debated in Parliament from a Home Office report. The mine was properly ventilated and the safety lamps were of a satisfactory design. Naked lights were used under certain and strict areas & conditions. The mine was not gaseous and no firedamp had been detected anywhere at the seat of the Explosion in the 'Low Main'. The causes of the explosion were very much discussed and debated over the following weeks if not months. 'The Home Office' report as already noted was put to Parliament. The mine was not exceptionally dusty but indeed well ventilated. No Firedamp had been found previously in the Low Main. It was pointed out that the Haulage Road out-bye was dustier than most other areas in the seam but this was due to coal coming off sets of tubs passing the area.

Eventually a theory was put forward that the coal dust in the air which could be a very inflammable mixture had been sparked off in some way causing the ignition. This may have been caused by a shot being fired improperly. T. Maddison fired the shot on this occasion; he had not been instructed to do this. His instructions were to clear a fall; not to remove a large obstruction in front of it. The shot firer had the most burns on his person; showing that the ignition commenced instantaneous with the shot and furthermore a cartridge was missing from Madison's supply; which was known to be in his possession. A spent piece of fuse wire was found close by. When the jury examined the area of the development they must of realised that the stone in the area had been blown not by the explosion but by the shot. Furthermore a shot on the main haulage way must have been found safe to fire a shot and would have been thought out of the way of Gas.

The H.M. Inspector of mines reached an opinion that the men including the shot firer were not aware of coal dust mixed with air were as lethal, as it turned out to be. They recommended that no further action should be taken against Management or any other party. Certain suggestions should be taken into account mainly to prevent this ever happening again 1/ the dangers of coal dust and air explosions should be circulated to Management and men. 2/ All shot firers should have the rules of shot firing printed on his authorisation form. 3/ That mine owners be made aware of dust blowing down shafts. 4/ That all main haulage roads henceforth be kept free of dust by watering or brushing.

A monument commemoration to the tragedy was unveiled just opposite the Church. Later in 1909 the Colliery was sold to the 'Weardale Coal Company', Sir Christopher Furness heading the group, the price being £175,000; the new manager was Charles Herbert Leeds.

Troubled Collieries

Because of the many men working in the pit at the time of the explosion scores of people came to the area of the Pit Head & waited for news of their loved one's. Below Wingate Main Street; unchanged over the years. Wingate Colliery was important to the area because of the employment it provided for the community:

Troubled Collieries

Above Funeral Procession 1896

Left Hutton Henry Up-Cast Shaft 1898

Victims of the Wingate Grange Colliery Explosion who died 14/10/1906

Name	Age	Occupation	Place of work
Victims in the field of the explosion in the Low Main seam			
Thomas Henry Elliott	46	shifter	At downcast shaft
John Thomas Maddison	24	stoneman	Engine plane to north
George Bloomfield	41	shifter	Engine plane Stable way
Victim near the field of the explosion in the Main Coal Seam			
John Guy Dixon	57	shifter	Near downcast shaft
Victims from after damp in the Low Main seam			
Alfred George Harris	50	shifter	Sump 2nd East way
Joseph Grafton	67	shifter	5th North 2nd East way
William Hockaday	51	sinker	Staple in West district
James Ainsley	20	pumper	2nd East way district
Charles Stockdale	35	sinker	,,
Thomas Bainbridge	66	examiner	1st East way
James Morrison	45	shifter	,,
Peter Gilchrist	63	shifter	,,
James Mason	49	stoneman	Water levels 2nd East way
Thomas Metcalfe	64	shifter	Sump 2nd East way
Thomas Kay	55	shifter	Water levels 2nd East way
Nathaniel Farnworth	59	shifter	
Henry Pace	44	stoneman	Longwall Stable way
Victims from after damp in the Main Coal Seam			
Isaac James	42	mason	Foot of incline to 5/4
Patrick Dunlavey	62	mason's labourer	,,
Victims from after damp in the Five Quarter seam			
George Smith	47	chargeman	Working in 5/4
Lord Bentley	66	shifter	,,
William Studham	54	shifter	,,
George Bayliss	58	examiner	,,
Edward Hardy	63	shifter	,,

Above is an official 'Home Office Report'.

Later on November 24th. George Mason died he was a shifter and had been in the Harvey seam at the time of the explosion and he died at home. This was initially reported as dyeing from Bronchitis but later death was found to be due to 'sub acute pneumonia', caused by cold, wet and exposure to the wet and cold. After a further six month James Pearse died reported to be because of the explosion. This amounted to a total of 26 sadly loosing their lives because of the Explosion:

EAST HETTON (Kelloe)
Inundation 1897

At 3.30 on May 6th. 1897, there was an inrush of water from old workings at East Hetton, Colliery. This caused an inundation when ten people lost their lives. There was one consolation in that there were only a small amount of people in the pit at this time; if it had happened in the day shift it would most certainly have cost more lives.

The first indication that all was not well occurred in the Harvey Seam. This was on the face of long wall workings, about a mile north of the shaft; water was noted coming from the forward coalface. Some men felt that this indicated danger and advised other workers to get away from the area. It would appear that if some of the men had not hesitated to put on their clothes they may have escaped with their lives. Among others that did escape from the Harvey at that time was David Galloway a well known local Methodist Lay Preacher.

The water quickly swamped the area and quickly rose to the roof; men tried to vacate the district by trying different routes towards the shaft. The water rose so fast that it cut them off and some were trapped. Two men saved themselves by keeping hold of the rope of the main haulage; although having water up to their necks they still managed to scramble to safety. Management of the Colliery finally were informed of the accident, Mr. Tate (Agent), Mr. Chipchase (Manager), over men, deputies and others quickly descended the pit. . Even at the shaft bottom, which was high ground the water, was three feet deep and it was found impossible to make any progress in bye.

Nearby there was an old Cassop shaft; this was situated about 300 yards from the long wall workings where the water was known to have breached the area of the coalface. Observant officials noticed that the water had receded here from its normal level. Years ago the Main Coal and Five Quarter seams were worked here. They were sure that they had holed into this source and they knew before the pumps could penetrate the water in the present seams that they would have to stop this feeder. "Get a plug in", as the saying goes. They were determined to stop this flow of water. A large engine house was knocked down and thrown into the shaft and sump area, clay, and soil lime anything that would stem water flow. Water tanks and pumps at East Hetton worked to capacity. Everyone waited anxiously. After a few hours the water began to drop in the shaft area and this was an indication that the plug in was working. Now only a small water feeder which the pumps could handle found its way into the forward areas.

Because the water had roofed in the present pit there had been a lack if not any air had reached forward areas and now gas was the problem. This had to be stabilized mainly by re-establishing air doors and again making air circulate to the inward areas. This had to be done before men could progress to the stricken areas. Managers and officials from other Collieries arrived at East Hetton; brave men up to their chests in water attempted to reach the entombed men, but again the water was still too deep for them to make any progress and they still had problems with falls of roof and also gas.

After two days they were at this time very pessimistic of finding any survivors. On the morning of the 10th. Mr. Chipchase heard a movement in the water some distance away from him. He rushed towards the sound as best he could still only half hoping that it may be a survivor; his second thought may be rats. The noise to his delight and surprise was a person coming towards him through the swirling water, which was still rather deep. The person was a deputy named Wilson; he struggled towards him hardly able to make progress with open arms and hugged the man; obviously weak with hunger and desperately cold and damp. The rescuers welcomed Wilson warmly, revived him with warm soup and brandy his cold and wet dirty pit clothing replaced with blankets. This brave Deputy had been imprisoned since 3 AM on the 6th. and it was estimated a total of 100 hours.

Mr. Wilson finding himself cut off climbed onto woodwork that was supporting horizontal sheaves which was connected to the haulage system. At this time the water was about 3 feet deep underneath him. He remained there half dazed; although he had chosen high ground there was water up to the roof either side of him. Wilson was grateful that the air left in the cavity had enough oxygen to keep him alive. He was very weak and it seemed that he drifted into long periods of sleep. The air in the cavity supported his life; but shortage of food gave him lapses of illusion when he fell into long periods of sleep and in his unconscious state he lost all track of time. He thought he had only been cut off 24 hours when infact he had been imprisoned 100 hours. When the water had receded enough he took the chance to get to safety.

There was an amazing coincidence concerning Mr. Wilson because he was the last person brought out alive from the Trimdon Grange pit after the explosion in 1882. With careful care by family and friends in the area; Wilson re-commenced his duties as a deputy within three months having no ill or after effects. The search went on for bodies in the pit and on the 12th. the first person was found and on the 13th. five more bodies were discovered. The final body was recovered on the 26th.May. 1897.

Everyone in the area of Kelloe, Quarrington Hill, Coxhoe and Cassop came together to help the poor families of the men who had lost their lives. Mr. Tate and Mr. Chipchase and all Colliery staff and workmen did their utmost at the Colliery. Viewers from neighboring Collieries were available constantly. Mr. Wilson, Mr. Johnson, and others from the 'Durham Miners Union', did not hesitate to search workings underground. The water had come in from old Cassop Colliery, but for a long period the reasons for the happenings remained unclear.

Falls of roof hindered exploration to find the area where they holed into the Old Cassop workings. It was estimated that 1000 tubs of debris and fallen stone from the roof; were removed from the area, this hardly cleared any way through. After heavy work in the area to reach the coalface, on the 18th. August they reached the area that had been holed. This laid to rest any other theory that may have caused the inundation. This was a clean hole that had been made into the old Cassop Shaft over 300 yards away.

The Colliery owners endeavored to make sure that all information were available on old workings. Drawings of the 'Five Quarter' and 'Main Coal' were readily available but no details were available of the Harvey Seam. Statements were taken from many people who were connected to the Colliery previously and it was found that they had driven only a short distance wrongly into the Cassop Shaft. This nevertheless was a costly mistake. **1/** Ten lives had been lost **2/** The Pecuniary losses to the Mining Company who owned the Colliery.

On further checking witnesses it was also found Mr. Bell, 30 years earlier had been connected with Cassop and was inspector in charge of this district was interviewed by Mr. Tate prior to the beginning of work in the Harvey seam and in his presence circled the working plan. This had a working 300-yard radius from the Cassop Pit. He told him that if he kept to the outside of the line, or if testing by boring they could infact go nearer with precautions. He again repeated this in evidence. A borehole was put in but this was to test for a fault that was known to be in the region of the seam and not to explore for the 'Old Cassop', shaft. He repeated the evidence before the Coroner and that if working was kept within the area laid down it would be perfectly safe. No old workings were anticipated to be in the area of the present Harvey seams. But what *is* certain is that more coal had been worked than he knew of.

Inquest

On the 1st. September after two adjournments the inquest went ahead and lasted two days. This ended in a verdict of 'Accidental Death'. The jury exonerated the Company and officials from all blame. Evidence were taken regarding previous workings in the Harvey Seam from the Cassop shaft. No evidence was forthcoming from any other source.

The inquest was held at a large schoolroom at Kelloe and it created much interest. The Company was represented by Mr. Stanton (Solicitor), of Newcastle and Mr. Atherley Jones QC. MP. Instructed by Mr. Isadore Issacs, represented the relatives of the deceased men. The Durham miners Association was represented by Mr. J. Wilson, MP, Mr. Foreman, Mr. Johnson and Mr. Cann.

It was found not necessary that Counsel should attend on behalf of the Home Office. The Jury after consulting about an hour returned the following verdict

Verdict

We find that Thomas Hutchinson and nine others accidentally lost their lives in the Harvey Seam at East Hetton Colliery by an accidental in rush of water from the old workings of the Harvey Seam of Cassop Colliery into the Harvey seam of the East Hetton Colliery on the morning of he 6th. day of May 1897. Further, we believe that Messrs. Chipchase and Tate did their best to find plans of the workings of the Old Colliery and we believe that they used every precaution for the safe working of the East Hetton Colliery, and we think no blame was attached to one or either of them.

The Coroner: were the jury unanimous? The Foreman replied **yes**.

The following is a list of the dead.
John Garside; aged 51, Stoneman, buried at St. Helens, Kelloe.
Anthony Gibbon; aged 41 Shifter.
William Hall; aged 50, Shifter.
Thomas Hutchinson, aged 49, Stoneman, buried at Quarrington Hill Churchyard.
James Oliver aged 42, Wasteman.
Edward Pearson aged 50 Wasteman.
John Raine, aged 63. Wasteman.
Matthew Robinson, aged 26, shifter.
Thomas Roney, aged 58, Shifter.
Edward Smith, aged 26, Shifter.

Lucky Escape~~~
Kelloe Colliery narrowly avoided a catastrophe in 1983 when due to observant officials hundreds of men were saved from inundation; Kelloe Colliery continued producing coal until 1989; but on the 24th. March 1983 it was planned to win high amounts of coal reserves found under Thornley. New roadways were developed and everything was made ready to work this coal it was said that many years of reserves of good coal waited to be developed. Officials at the Colliery for some reason became suspicious of water situated above the seam. The Busty at the time lay 90 feet below an old Tilley seam of Thornley Colliery. As the seam had been originally dry no water problems had been envisaged. To confirm this checks were never the less still made. On the 29th. March drilling was commenced into the old Tilley seam; when reaching 112 feet on the 19th. April contact was made with the Tilley goaf, the drill was 15 mm, water began to flow but was soon blocked. The hole was then reamed and a pressure gauge fitted a reading registered 68 lbs /sq. inch, this reading astonished the officials. Mr. Dunbar ordered a change of gauge and this confirmed the high reading. It meant that above them was 162 feet head of water. The entire Thornley Tilley seam and the Harvey above it was filled with 173 million gallons of water. The order was quickly given for all of the men to be withdrawn from the area.

Troubled Collieries

Two views of the famous **_St. Helens Church_** at Kelloe where Elizabeth Barrett Browning was christened in 1806 when she was born at nearby Coxhoe Hall. Many services were held here for the **_Kelloe Men_** and boys who were killed in the Explosion & the Inundation; nearby is the Memorial pictured below that records all of the dead: *Photograph's 'The Author':*

Troubled Collieries

Above **_Kelloe Colliery_** one of the greatest producing Collieries in Durham: **Kelloe Village**, below showing the road leading to old Town Kelloe, lower down the Institute where many functions were organised and many football teams changed; later because of Quarry developments Town Kelloe was deserted.

MINING TERMS USED IN THE BOOK

Viewer & Resident Viewer.
Probably the most important man in the Coal Industry. He advised owners, Management, and everyone else in all aspects of Mining and Colliery Life. As well as the viability. Some Viewers were resident some had other interests in ownership and advising investing share holders. All had been available from the very start of that particular Colliery; were mainly well known like Mr. Humble, Mr. Buddle and Mr John Robson the latter was owner and part owner in many Collieries and actually advised the 'Clarence Railway' in the purchase of Collieries.

Master Shifter
Was overall in charge of the pit, in any paricular shift usually an expert on all aspects of mining.

Shaft................................*Where miners waited to get the cage to transport them to the surface, or into the pit.*

Keps..........*At each seam there was keps automaticaly placed under the cage to allow the men to come out of the cage safely.*

Bank.......................*Surface of the Colliery.*

In bye.....................*Towards the workings or coal face*

Out bye....................*towards the shaft.*

Chumming....................*Empty Tub.*

Set.........................*A number of Tubs coupled together to transport coal to the shaft and then to the surface.*

Deputy..........................*In charge of men down the pit, usually measured work and in charge of general every day organization.*

Shot Firer........*Responsible for firing the shots of explosive after drilling, a good shot firer could help a filler tremendously in making sure the coal was properly fired and broken up.*

Overman.....................*Overall control of the area or seam responsible to the Manager.*

Scythe....................... *Usually present in the air after shots are fired or when air is not circulating properly.*

Conveyor Belt...................*Continuous system to take coal to the surface of the Colliery from the coal face.*

Face................................*Coal Face where coal was taken out of the Strata, many having names like Harvey or Busty, some coal seams were better quality than others, and used for making coke and other by-products.*

Goaf............................*The area where the coal was taken out of the strata, this had to be dropped to take the strain off the continuous process of winning the coal and at times this was extremely hazardous.*

Gasses...........................*Firedamp, Afterdamp, Blackdamp, all types of gas that was present mainly in pockets within the strata or goaf in the pit, a good miner could identify which gas was present. Every miner carried a testing lamp in the pit, which showed the percentage present, if there was a high amount present, then the area was evacuated.*

Main & Tail....................*Haulage System where chains were fastened in front and behind, to a haulage rope pulling a set of two tubs, these were easily disconnected from the system and the coal disposed of at the surface.*

Endless. *This was the endless haulage rope used for the above system.*

Putter.... *Responsible for supplying chumming and taking away full tubs of coal, forming them into a set to be transported to the shaft*

Galloway Putter *the same as above but with a pony. This could be extremely hazourdous two of the Authors friends were involved in very bad incidents involving pit ponies; both incidents happening at Tursdale Colliery, Co. Durham. Hugh Bryden from New Durham was killed when riding the pony out bye at the end of a shift. A roof girder had dropped during the shift just a matter of a few inches. Bobbie Brown from Park Hill, Nr. Bowburn was badly injured when he was kicked by a pony*

Sinker............*Shaft Sinkers, the start of the Colliery to locate and sink into a major seam of coal*

Resident Viewer...*Respected Mining expert who gave advise to Management for the safe running of the Colliery*

Kist ...... *Where all men gathered before a shift to be given instructions on the day's duties*

Downcast Shaft...*Where fresh air entered the Colliery*

Up cast Shaft.........*where the used and stale air was disposed of usually through a high chimney*

drawing the cage up and down the shaft.
Wagon Way...*The main road to the shaft where coal was transported*
Wagon Way Man...*One of the most important men underground, responsible for the smooth running of the sets and coal, rails, haulage equipment and ropes, even splicing and joining wire ropes. If there was a hold up in production away from the coal faces then he was the one that sorted the problem out.*
Hewers...*Manually produce coal from an uncut face of coal usually on faces which were being developed, their main tool was a bull pick.*
Canaries. ...*Were used to test for gas every Colliery had them and usually kept them near to shafts on the surface, were very sensitive to gas and other fumes.*
On Setter.........*Responsible for the smooth running of the shaft area and Cage for transporting men and coal out and in to the pit. They also carefully searched men for counterfeit smoking facilities and also checked that safety lamps were properly locked.*
Drillers...*Drilled the coalface prior to being shot fired with explosive.*
Cutter Man...*Cut the bottom of the seam of coal so that when fired it was easily filled on to belts.*
Filler.........*It was his job to fill a measured amount of coal from a face each day after it had been drilled cut and fired; their main tool was an extra large shovel.*
Dregs...*Used to stop full tubs and sets arriving at the shaft bottom from in bye, prior to transporting to the surface. A good landing lad could throw up to six dregs Accurately into the wheels of a moving set to stop it.*
Token .... *As a secondry check on who was in the pit and who was not, each miner was given a token with a number on, so that at the lamp cabin each person's whereabouts were known at once. Initially at Stanley it was not known exactly how many men were involved.*
Cavilling.......... *Each quarter good and bad duties were drawn fairly, this was to allow the work to be fairly shared.*

Troubled Collieries

Present Day Safety Equipment

The Concordia Cap Lamp, the battery is carried on the miners waist belt and the lamp clips on to the hard hat. The light brings a different dimension to seeing underground; as the shift expires the battery is plugged into a charging system that ensures that the lamp is ready for next shift:

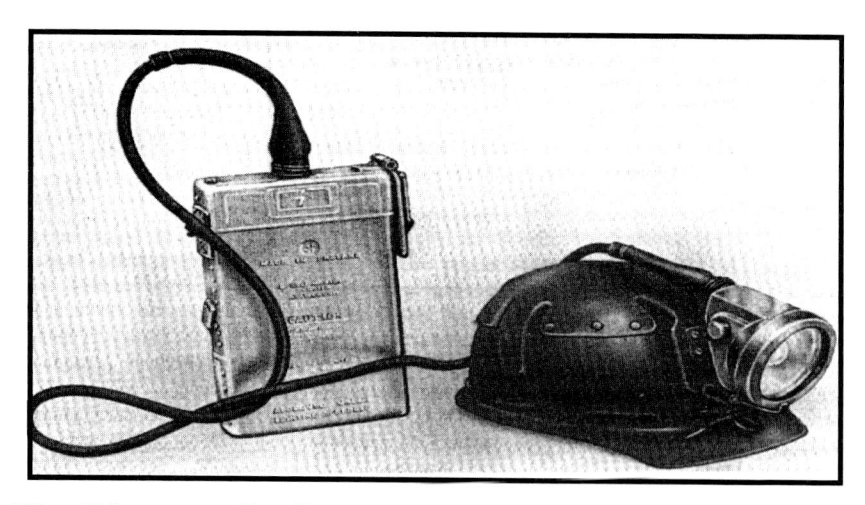

The Ringrose Gas Detector, showing component parts; it was compulsory to carry a lamp when going underground, at the shaft top, they were checked making sure the lamp was locked; a check was also made for contraband. The lamp showed five percent fire damp gas when there was a danger of an explosion:

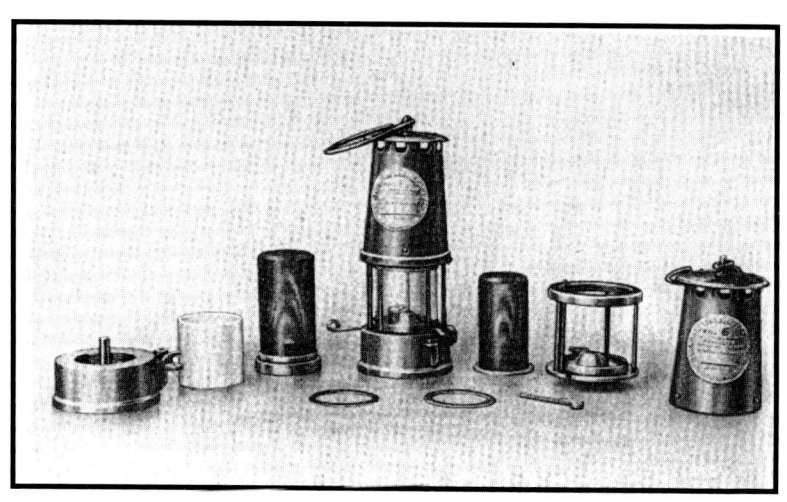

Name & Place Index

A
Aberdare 54
Accidental death 132
Adams Bill 16
Afterdamp 34
Air Crossings 60.
Algernon Most Noble 24
Amour 10, 19.
Anderson Henry 91,92,93.
Armstrong Hugh 59.
Armstrong Jimmy 97.
Armstrong Thomas 59.
Armstrong Tommy 97.
Armstrong Works 66.
Artus Robert 58.
Ashcroft 124.
Ashington 104.
Atkinson Bros 65.
Atkinson D. 118.
Atkinson Family 72.
Atkinson J.B. 73,75,76.
Atkinson W.N. 45, 53, 55.
Atlee Earl 88.
August 23
Aukland Park 120.
Australia 74.
Aycliffe Village 109.

B
Baglin J.59.
Bain Donald 71.
Bankhead 44.
Barber & Co. 32.
Barker 38.
Barnsley 7, 32, 36, 41.
Barometric 35.
Barrett Elizabeth 134
Beamish 76.
Beddows Rev. 109.
Bell Mr. 131.
Benwell 72.
Bewick Bob. 10.
Binchester 120.
Bird William 115.
Birtley 66.

Bishop Aukland 15.
Bishop Lightfoot 59.
Bishop of Durham 67, 98, 109, 125.
Bitchburn 120.
Blackburn Henry 84, 88.
Blackett Charles 73.
Blackett Colonel 70.
Blackett W.C. 66.71.
Blackett William 83, 87.
Blackwell 22.
Blenkinsop Thomas 95.
Blyth &Tyne Railway 25.
Bolden 114.
Botanic 52.
Bowes George 59.
Boyne Lord 119.
Brancepeth Colliery 106, 114.
Brandling William 90.
Brandon 116.
Brass John 85, 86.
Brennan Louis 109.
Brennan Michael 109.
British 51.
British Forces 109.
Brockwell 68, 73, 74, 115, 116.
Brown Doctor 118.
Brown James 46.
Brown Samuel 38.
Browning 134.
Bruce Doctor Dr. 20.
Burdess Henry 106.
Burnett Crescent 97.
Burnett James 97.
Burnett Joseph 97.
Burnett Mrs. 98.
Burns John 59.
Burns Pit 65, 75.
Burton Ted. 73.
Busty 70, 74, 75, 123.
Byron Pit 82.

C
'Cresford' 108.
Cairns Michael 58.
Cairns Robert 58.

141

Name & Place Index

Cairns Sam 98.
Cambrian Lamp 55.
Cannon Body 71.
Captain 84, 86.
Carbonic Acid 13.
Cardiff 54.
Carling Tom. 119.
Carr Bros. & Co. 25.
Carr Charles 18.
Carr Mr. 17, 45, 74.
Carr William 74.
Cassop 129, 131.
Catholic Church 72, 73, 119.
Cemetery 60.
Chairman N.C.B. 107.
Chapman T. 59.
Charlaw & Sacriston Coal Company 83.
Charlaw Colliery 83.
Chaytor William 73.
Cherry 59.
Chester le Street 82.
Chesterfield 35.
Chipchase Mr. 129, 132.
Chivers E. 120.
Choke Damp Gas. 35.
Christmas 33, 34, 41.
Chronicle 34, 36.
Church of England 108.
Church Yard 20 133.
Clanny Safety Lamp 46.
Clark Henry 70.
Clergymen 37.
Coal Company 126.
Coal Mines 23.
Cobb Colonel 35.
Coking Works 114.
Coldstream Guards 109.
Coldwell 61.
Cole Mr. 47.
Colliery Engineer 67.
Colliery Manager 44.
Colonel Blackett 66, 70, 71.
Commission of accidents 40.
Consolidated Mining 51.

Cook Thomas 58.
Cook William 117.
Cook's 59.
Cornsay Colliery 85.
Coroner 22, 45, 65, 74, 132.
Coroner Graham 70, 71.
Cotton George 35.
Coulson William 5, 8, 9, 12, 13, 14, 17, 18, 21, 22, 23, 42, 65, 67, 123,
Coundon 120.
Counsel 132.
Cousins Thomas 16.
Cowpen 18, 20.
Cox H. F. Mr. 116, 120.
Coxhoe 131.
Coxhoe Hall 134.
Cramlington 18, 20.
Cricket Club 119.
Crook 105, 116..
Cross Cut 95. 120
Cross Streets 83.
Croxdale 59.
Crumlin 54.
Cummings John, 109.
Cuncliffe 125.
Cunningham Thomas 115.
Curry William 59.
Curve 43, 46.
Cutter Machine 103.

D

'Dead March in Saul'87.
'Dead March' 72.
Daisy Drift 115.
Daisy Hill 84.
Dalziel Phillip 59.
Davies M.J. 119.
Davison Doctor 24.
Dean & Chapter 90.
Dean Bridge 56.
December 39, 40.
Deneside 106.
Deputies 91.
Deputies Kist 105.
Deputy 36.

Troubled Collieries

Name & Place Index

Dickinson Joseph 39, 40.
Dickie J.P. M.P. 76.
Dobson John 123.
Dobson Thomas 43.
Doctor 45.
Doctor Brown 118.
Doctor Bruce 20.
Doctor Garson 87.
Doctor Sam Watson 88.
Douglas E. 119, 120.
Dowdell 59.
Ducham Baron 24.
Duckbill District 6, 103, 108, 109.
Duke of Kent 82.
Dunkirk 104.
Dunn Matthias 32.
Durham 7. 24, 94, 109.
Durham Coalfields 109.
Durham Miners Association 119.
Diamond Thomas 34, 35.

E

Eagle D. 59.
Easington 46, 61, 103, 104, 105, 107, 108, 109, 110.
Easington Colliery 6, 7.
East Hetton 95, 96, 130, 131, 132, 133.
East Side 53.
East Way 125.
Eddie George 59.
Eden William 119.
Edwards E. 59.
Elliot Matthew 57.
Elliott Sir George 38.
Elliott Street 86.
Embleton T. 38.
Emerson George 8, 16, 24.
Engine Man 115.
Engineer 67.
England 82.
Etherley 120.
Explosion 119.

F

Farnworth 125.
Farridge John 59.

Farrow Mr. G. 119.
Fat Nelly's 82.
Faulkner Joseph 58, 61.
February 22.
Felling 90, 94.
Felling Colliery 7. 90
Firebricks 123.
Firedamp 39, 103, 109, 126.
Five Quarter 82, 125. 132
Flemming William 118.
Foreman Mr. 133
Forester 84, 85.
Foster Joseph 116, 119.
Fulforth District 84.
Funeral 19.119
Furness Sir Christopher 127.

G

Gair Jonathan 59.
Gallagher John. 22.
Galway fiddles 83.
Garner 69.
Garside Doctor 87.
Garside John 134.
Gateshead 90.
Generation Trust 110.
Gibbon Anthony 134.
Gilchrist John 116.
Gilmore Sir John 76.
Governments 20, 24, 120.
Graham Coroner 65, 70, 71, 74.
Graham John 87.
Greener 91.
Greener T.Y. 120.
Grieves Mr. 115, 116.

H

Haig Matthew 36.
Halifax Viscount 37.
Hall J.P. 66.
Hall John. 88.
Hall William 134.
Handel 72.
Hanson 117.
Harcourt Sir William 45.
Harrison Bob 69.

Troubled Collieries

Name & Place Index

Hartley 5, 9, 20, 21, 22.
Hartley Colliery 18, 23, 25.
Harvey 45, 95, 96, 124, 130, 134.
Hastings Lord 21.
Haswell William 91, 92.
Headway 96.
Hell Pit 44.
Henderson & Grace 90.
Henderson Mark 69, 70, 71.
Hendy C. 120.
Henry J. Hodgeson 117.
Hett Whin Dyke 60.
Hetton Coal Company 42.
Heugh Edge 84.
Hewers 97.
Heworth 90.
High & Low pits 43.
High Main 9, 11, 12, 13.
High Pit 44, 48.
History 120.
Hockin S. 59.
Hockin W. 59.
Hodgeson 67.
Holmeside Colliery 76.
Holsten Father 119.
Home Secretary 21, 54, 76.
Hopkinson Mr. 120.
Houghton Le Spring 104.
Houram John 35.
House of Lords 74, 76.
Hoyland 38.
Hudson's Railway Shares 76.
Humble Joseph 21.
Hunt Stephen 106.
Hutchinson 35, 43.
Hutchinson Thomas 133, 134.
Hutton 46.
Hyndley Lord. Lord 107.

I
Indian William 75.
Inspector of Mines 126.
Institute of Chemistry 46.
Irish Row 83.
Irvine David 98.

Isaacs Isadore 133

J
Keegan Frank 71.
Kelloe 7, 96, 132, 133, 134, 135.
Kimberley 52.
King 68.
Kings Head 38.
Kirkup F.O. 119.

L
Labour Government 6.
Ladysmith 52.
Lambton Arms 82.
Lambton John 59.
Lambton William 58.
Lancaster 52.
Landlord 44.
Law Courts 54.
Laws Mr. 115.
Laws William 118.
Lawson Charles 43.
Lawson John 59.
Lawson Mr. 115
Lawson Ralph 117.
Lawson Thomas 117.
Lawther G. W. 118.
Leeds 127.
Lewins 57.
Lewis Merthyr 51.
Lintern Charles 118.
London 16, 40, 94.
Londonderry family 48.
Londonderry Institute 45.
Lord Boyne 119.
Lord Hastings 21, 25.
Lord Hyndley 107.
Lord Joicey 76
Lord Lawson 76.
Lord Mayor 40.
Louisa Colliery 65.
Love Joseph 114.
Low Main 13, 90, 95, 97, 123, 126.
Luke Tommy 123.
Lundill Pit 35.

M

Troubled Collieries

Name & Place Index

'*March in Saul*' 87.
'Mines & Miners ' 20.
Madison T. 126.
Mafeking District 55.
Mafeking Kimberley 52.
Magnesium Limestone 123.
Main & Tail 95.
Main Coal 44, 45, 82, 104, 130, 132.
Majesty 18.
Majesty The Queen 37.
Mammatt J. E. 32, 38, 39.
Management 69, 96.
Manager 68, 70, 71, 105, 119, 131.
Manchester 32.
Marquis of Londonderry 42.
Masons 91.
Master General 60.
Master Shifter 124.
Master Sinker 8, 13, 24, 123.
Master Waste Man 95.
Maudling Seams 45.
Maughan John 59.
Mc Gunnel H. 125.
Mc Kenna 54.
McCormick Patrick 87.
McCormick Thomas 86, 87.
Meadowfield 114.
Memorial 135.
Menham Michael 91.
Methodist 8, 108.
Milburn 11. 59
Mine Banner 88.
Mine Inspectors 45.
Mining Company 132.
Mining Engineer 84.
Minto 35.
Mitchell Joseph 59.
Monologue 67.
Morgue 118.
Morley Arnold 60.
Morton 32.
Most Noble Algernon 24.
Mount Etna 91.
Murton Colliery 42.

Mutton J. 59.

N

Naisbit 58.
Narrow Board 95, 97.
National Coal Board 56.
Newcastle upon Tyne 18, 66, 68, 73, 76, 97, 133.
Newell Bartholomew 116.
Newton Cap 120.
Nicholson Thomas 116, 119.
Nicky Knack 43, 60.
Nonconformist Church 72.
North Country 124.
North Country Woman 120.
North Flat 84.
North Of England 20.
Northumberland 7, 8.
November 54, 65, 83.

O

Oakenshaw 114, 116.
Oaks Colliery 39, 40.
Oakum 94.
Old Cassop 132.
Old Sharpe 10, 11.
Oliver James 134.
Osborne 18.
Our Lady of Perpetual Succor 119.
Overmen 91.

P

Palmer Sir Charles. 125.
Parish Council 110.
Parish of Heworth 90
Parkin John 73.
Parliament 126.
Patterson William 57.
Pearson Edward 134.
Pearson Joseph 91, 92.
Peart John 70.
People 41.
Phillips Theo. Coun. 119.
Phipps C. B. 19.
Pit Head 43, 123.
Pit John 90.
Pit Owners 20.

Name & Place Index

Pit Shaft 21.
Plane Board 93.
Porth Rescue Services 52.
Post Master General 60.
Presbyterian 119.
President of the Institute of Chemistry 46.
Primitive Methodist Chapel 19.
Primitive Methodists 119.
Prudential 119.

Q

Quarrington Hill 132, 134
Queen Victoria 17, 18, 45, 82.

R

Rafter George 105.
Raine John 134.
Ramshaw 46.
Red Cross 54.
Resident Viewer 21.
Rhondda 54.
Rhymner James 58.
Rhymney Valleys 54.
Richard Joseph 58.
Richardson Robert 86, 87.
Riley Tom 67.
Ritchie Ronnie 103.
Rivers Michael 59.
Roberts Edward Jones 59.
Robinson Matthew 134.
Robson Ralph 9, 12.
Robson Rev. M.M. 119.
Roderidge Firebricks 123.
Rodgers John 73.
Rogers Edward 91, 92.
Rogerson John 116.
Roman Catholics 108.
Roney Thomas 134.
Royal Commission 38.
Royal Oak 7.
Rutherford 44.
Rutherford John 115.
Rutter Matthew 59.

S

Sacriston 66, 82, 83, 84, 85.
Sacriston Victoria 7.
Saint Robert 108.
Salvation Army 69, 108.
Saturday 71.
Schier H.C. 95, 97.
Scott Walter 97.
Seaham 42, 43, 46, 47, 56.
Seaham Colliery 44, 47, 48, 67.
Seaton High Pit 42.
Seaton Sluice 25.
Seghill 20.
Senghenydd 7, 45, 51.
Sharpe Billy 12.
Sharpe John 16.
Sharpe William 10, 11.
Shaw 52.
Shaw Edward 53.
Sheffield Railway 32.
Shields Billy 8.
Shieldsfield District 58, 161.
Shinwell 107.
Short John 21.
Shotfirers 105.
Simenon 20.
Singapore 109.
Sinkers 16, 19.
Slogget Henry 58.
Smith 36, 37.
Smith Edward 134.
Smith Ernie 70.
Smith Michael 47.
Smith William 59, 70.
Snowden Thomas 59.
South Moor 76.
South Shields 82, 114.

T

Taffenel M. 70.
Tate Mr. 132.
Tate Simon 88.
Taylor John 21.
Ternant Thomas 16.
The Tilley 69.
Theatre Royal 66.

Troubled Collieries

Name & Place Index

Thomas & Williams 55.
Thompson Thomas 57.
Thompson William 58.
Thorley Charles 35.
Thorneycroft 104.
Thornley 116, 120, 134.
Tilley 134.
Tindall George 57.
Townley 70, 74, 75.
Trimdon 68, 96.
Trimdon Grange 7, 97, 98, 132.
Tudhoe 7, 115.
Tudhoe Lane 60, 61.
Turnbull James 92.
Turnbull Robert 18.
Turner Michael 116.
Turning the Tide 110.
Tyne & Wear 94.
Tyne Docks 82.
Tyneside 94.

U
Under Manager 95.
Unison 110.
Urwin William 59.

V
Victoria Crosses 38.
Victoria Seam 75, 84.
Viewers 132.
Volunteer Infantry 84.
Volunteers 107.

W
Wagon Way Man 103.
Waldridge 82.
Wales 7.
Wallace J.G. 59.
Wallace T. Y. 106.
Wards William 35.
Washington & Durham Railway 114.
Washington Glebe 6. 72.
Waste Man 92.
Watson Dr. Sam.
Watson E. 119.
Watson Rev. 67.

Watson Tom 9, 10, 11.
Weardale Coal Company 59, 60. 126.
Wearmouth John 117.
Weeks Mr. 115. 116
Wellington 72 118..
Welsh Valleys 51.
Wesleyan Chapel 119.
West Level 55.
West Pit 60.
West Stanley 56.
White Lee 120.
Whitehaven 72.
Whittaker Bobby 84.
Whittaker John 86, 87.
Widdes C. 119.
Wilkinson Anthony 119.
Wilkinson Davy 8.
William 72.
William Pit 90, 93.
Williams Mattie 107.
Willington 114, 120.
Wilson George 115.
Wilson John M.P. 91 116.
Wilson Mr. 131, 132, 133.
Wilson Robert 16.
Wilson Thomas.
Wingate 6.
Wingate Grange 72 123.
Wonfor W. 119.
Wood Stephen 70.
Woodhorn 72.
Woodhouse John Thomas 32, 35.
Wraith H. 59.
Wyon Mr. 23.

Y
Yorkshire 32.
Yorkshire Post 33, 36.
Young Dick 124.

The Stanley Monologue

My family were always proud of the part Grandfather 'William Coulson', played in helping the poor miners at Stanley. Coulson died 15th April 1917. Prematurely Aged 58. Health wise he was never well again after the injuries sustained after the Explosion at Stanley. Just prior to his death he put down a Monologue on paper which was in my Mothers possession. His Granddaughter Ida learned this off by heart and recited it at gatherings (especially 'British Legion'). In later years her family the Heslington's learned the Monologue. Each member recited a number of verses; but no one penned it and unfortunately it died with my sister Ida. I am including in the book two 'Monologues', both very well written the first by Michael Bailey; a Deputy at the 'Margaret Pit and who sadly died May 19th. 1998 aged 67. the second by 'James Thompson', from South Shields who in 1909 sold copies at One penny with proceeds for the relief fund. These were sent to me by Robert A. Drake from Stanley who still works hard to make sure this terrible tragedy is never forgotten at present he is involved with Sue Coults in finding the last resting place of some of the brave men; with help from Kevin Keegan and 'The Northern Echo'.

Troubled Collieries

THE TRADGEDY OF THE MINE

The sixteenth of February ninteenhundred and nine,
Was a dreadful day, at West Stanley Mine,
That afternoon at quarter to four,
A hundred and sixty eight lives, were to be no more, A thunderous roar, through the town rang, Fifty seconds later, came the big bang,
Everyone in Stanley, just froze for a bit,
They knew there was trouble at Burns Pit,
Eye witnesses who had been standing close by,
Said the flames from the shaft had lit up the sky,
The whole town made their way to the pit head,
Not knowing then how many were dead,
As darkness fell the frost glistened bright,
They knew this would be a very long night,
Someone in the crowd said *Isn't it strange,*
It's the anniversary of the explosion at Trimdon Grange.
A small girl sobbed while saying a prayer,
Please Lord help me, my dad's down there,
Also down there, are my two brothers,
And its only a year since the death of my Mother.
After eight hours waiting came a wonderful thing,
The Tilley seam telephone started to ring,
Mark Henderson called *there's twenty six of us here,*
That news made the crowd give a tremendous cheer.
Hendersns bravery, meant these men were alive,
He'd led them to safety in groups of five,
The rescures toiled underground,
Till no more survivors could be found,
To have no father was many childrens fate,
Tommy Riley had eleven bairns, Luke Reay had eight,
The boy McGarry's body was found,
Hed gone down with his dad, to have a look around,
Why he'd been down there, made people wonder
He wasn't due to start work, till the following Monday,
The search was abandoned, for Rogers and Chaytor,
their remains were found, twenty four years later.
To remember these miners as each year goes, Just think of a pack of dominoes,
Using this method, they wont be forgot,
 Each victim represented by a spot.
Those men and boys , endured great pain,
Yet the loss of their lives, had not been in vain,The Town was denuded of a generation,
But if forced the coal owners into new legislation.
In some homes in Stanley every Tuesday,
It is still referred to as bad news day,
Those miners went to work full of mirth,
And were all destroyed in the bowels of the earth.

**By
Michael Bailey**

Troubled Collieries

Stanley Memorial Poem

Oh, weird the tale these lines relate,
And keenly speaks misfortune great,
That justice well may vindicate
For common weal;
And to the man of high estate,
A strong appeal.

The wintry sun had dragged itsground,
And darkness strove to veil theground,
A deadening quiet reigned profound ,
A wonderous still;
When lo! A dull and becoming sound
Predicting ill.

The active ear in musics charm,
Is swift to catch the first alarm,
That points or leads to future harm,
To friendship dear;
The hearts that's with effection warm
Will flame in fear.

The deaf'ening thud again repeats,
And echoes loud through Stanley streets,
Its mystic origin defeats
The native wit;
One moment more the truth completes
And wonders flit.

Yon gloomy mine, the precints near
Has been the source of doubt and fear,
But now its awful doom is clear
In briefest time;
It fills the clammy atmosphere
With smoke and grime.

Where is my husband ? Where my son?
That has my deep effection won,
What have I here to rest upon
Except their love?
Ah! What of me if they're undone,
I fail to move.

Where is my aged father ? Say!
With drooping head & locks of grey,
Who led me on from day to day
In paths of right;
Forbid he's viewed the parting ray
Of earthly light.

They now recall the parting kiss,
The stamp that seals all humane bliss,
When duty calls us to dismiss
For one short day;
The future unrevealing this
Should be for aye.

No tongue could half the misery tell,
No eye portray that sombre spell,
No ear define the lingering knell,
That counts the dead;
Unless that he in Stanley dwell,
By honour led.

While eyes with glistening tears are wet,
The picture is in memory set,
No feeling heart could e'er forget,
So weird a view,
In fitful dreams I see it yet,
And weep it through

In final words, may time covey
A tide of peace to soothe their way,
May joy replace the sad dismay,
Let hope enshrine;
Tho memory holds that fatal day,
God will devine.

Selected verses from the Memorial Poem. By James Thompson (Shields)

Mr R A DRAKE.
7 Belle Street.
Stanley
Co Durham.
D H 9-0DB.

12/3/2004.

Dear Bernard.

I forward for your keeping the two Memorial Poems, relating to the "West Stanley Colliery Disaster" of Feb 16th 1909. As you will see James Thompson of South Shields wrote one of the Poems at the time of the Disaster and Michael Bailey of Stanley penned the other many years later. Michael at one time was a Deputy at the Margaret Pit at Tanfield Lea, near Stanley. He took a major part in raising funds for the erection of a Memorial to the victims of that Horrendous Tragedy. The Unveiling of the Memorial was carried out on Feb 16th 1995 at 3:45pm by Kevan Keegan the then manager of Newcastle United Football Club. Unfortunately on May 19th 1998 Michael Bailey died, aged 67 years.

I only hope that the information I have forwarded to you meets with your requirements.

Best of Luck with the 2nd Edition of your Book

Yours Sincerely
Robert A Drake.

Troubled Collieries

Manchester City Plc

KK/JMcC

13th June 2002

Bernie McCormick
16 Cheviot Place
Newton Aycliffe
Co Durham
DL5 7EL

Dear Bernie

Thank you for your letter and very kind words of congratulations on our promotion.

I will be only too pleased to be added to your sponsor list and please let me know when you want my cheque forwarding to you.

Good luck with the book launch in August, I am sure it will be a success and a great tribute to those who perished or were badly injured in pit disasters, and the families who suffered.

Kind regards

Yours sincerely

Kevin Keegan
Manager

Chairman, D.A.Bernstein
Directors, C.M. Bird // B. Bodek // A.M. Lewis // A.J. Mackintosh // D. Tueart // J.C. Wardle
General Secretary, J.B. Halford

Registered in England. Registered No. 2989498

Bernard McCormick worked at Bowburn Colliery after leaving Cornforth Lane School. After five years he left the pits and completed his National Service with the 13/18 Royal Hussars, in Malaya during the Emergency where he saw active service. After Being demobbed he married, his wife Eileen, then Worked twenty years in Engineering. Later he ran a successful designer Clothing Business. Bernie, now retired writes extensively on Family and Local History. He has written four books on Northern and Scottish characters in the Northern and Scottish Folk series, and has researched, written and edited his family history, which includes four families. Bernard has also written books on North East mining, including 'Troubled Collieries', which was a great success especially in the North East; and which he is reprinting again, & includes four more Collieries and an extra fifty pages. Bernard is researching the Coulson's & Robson's on his mother's side, Jane Fletcher Coulson, who were all Colliery owners & shaft sinkers.

Bernie has written and published a pictorial group of books on Coxhoe and district where he was born. A book not yet published is 'The Pease Dynasty', which traces the early beginnings of the S&D Railway at Darlington and the people involved in establishing this brilliant time in North East History.

In 2003 Bernard signed a Contract with 'Business Education Publishers Limited', *(Leighton),* to produce 'Northern Folk 1 & 2 as one volume of 24 stories of Northern Characters:

Troubled Collieries SUBSCRIBER LIST

Kevin Keegan, Manager, Manchester City, F.C.
Mr. & Mrs. B. McCormick, Newton Aycliffe.
Mr. & Mrs. Paul Ackley, Newton Aycliffe.
Darren & Alison, Hetton.
www.wizzegroup.com, Web site design Newton Aycliffe,
Ernie O'Keefe, Ripon.
Barry Heslington, Coxhoe.
Harry Wilson, Bogma Avenue, Coxhoe.
Eileen Bryan, Grange Cres., Coxhoe.
L.H. Gardner, Stanley.
Robert Facey, Low Willington.
M.W. Foreman, Stanley.
E. Livingstone, Stanley.
James Kirkley, South Shields.
Ken Robinson, Telford.
David Worthington, Croxdale, Durham.
Mr. J.B. Stephenson, Witton Gilbert.
F.E. & Mr. Laing, Newsagent, Coxhoe.
Mr. Derrick Scott, Springwell, Gateshead.
Rev. John Stephenson, New Herrington, Sunderland.
Fred & Jean Phillips, Dover, Kent.
Mr. & Mrs. R.J. Robinson, Coxhoe.
Miss Ivy Barkhouse, Knowe Park Avenue, Carlisle.
Mr. R. A. Drake, Stanley.
Doctor Stephenson, Surgery , Newton Aycliffe.
Judge A.R.Elliott, C/o Scarborough C.C. Yorkshire.
Mr& Mrs. L. McCormick Millfield, Aycliffe Village.
Mr. & Mrs. S. McCormick, Egton Way, Darlington.
Mary & John Moran, Bede Crescent, Newton Aycliffe, Co. Durham.
Liam Kemp, www.wizzegroup.com.
John Lawrence www.wizzegroup.com.
M.W. Foreman, Craghead, Stanley.
E. Livingston, Craghead, Stanley.
Mr. R. Lomas, Stillington, York.
Mr. & Mrs. Frank Taylor, Linden Grove, Coxhoe, Co. Durham.
John Taylor, Wick Lane, Colchester,
Mrs. Joyce Taylor, Conifer Close, Colchester.
Mr.& Mrs. Ronnie Taylor, Sedgefield.
Mr.& Mrs B. Hilton, Scarborough, North Yorks.

David P. Worthington, Croxdale, Durham.
Charles Bartlett Heslington, Westcott Terrace, Ferryhill,
Tony Brewster, Garrage, Aycliffe Industrial Estate.
Mr. Harry & Mrs. Ann Trevor, Scholars Path, Newton Aycliffe.
Mr.& Mrs. Ernie Gardner, Newtredagar, South Wales.
Mr.& Mrs. John & Kate Wilkinson, Warminster, Wiltshire.
Mr. & Mrs. Paul Goundry, Hunwick.
David Fletcher, Newton Aycliffe.
Mr. Denis Ackley, Durham Road, Spennymoor.
Michael Ackley, Durham Road, Spennymoor.
Kathrine Ackley, Kirk Merrington, Co. Durham.
Louise & Jed. Crossen, Newton Aycliffe.
Mary & John Moran, Bede Crescent, Newton Aycliffe, Co. Durham.
Colin & Louise, Moran, Wakefield.
Jack Trowell, Ferryhill Broom, Ferryhill.
Mr. & Mrs. Susan & Neil Davies, Old School House, Toad Lane
Mr. & Mrs. Valerie & Roy Lee, Medina Drive, Tollerton.
Robert Robinson, The Grove, Coxhoe, Co. Durham.
Thomas Ord Blenkinsop, & Edith Blenkinsop, 10, Whitwell Terrace.
Vera & Colin, Spennymoor, Co. Durham.
Jack Trowell, Ferryhill Broom, Ferryhill.
Brian McGowan, The Grove, Coxhoe, Co. Durham.